As someone who loves dining at the bar when I go out, *Belly Up to the Bar* is the perfect alternative to the usual restaurant guide. Restaurant eviewers often overlook the joys of bar dining; here is a reminder, with a reat selection of restaurants, that one can be more spontaneous and asual at the bar while eating great food and getting good service.

Wylie Dufresne, Chef/ Co-owner
wd~50 (Michelin ★)

My favorite pastimes are eating, drinking, and talking about eating and drinking, and this book does it all.

Jimmy Bradley, Chef/Owner
The Harrison and The Red Cat

When I placed the first crisp white oversized napkin out on the Café des Artistes mahogany bar in 1975, a new American tradition was born; warm café hospitality married upscale dining. How lucky we are that J. S. Mitchell loves the idea, because Mitchell has written such a charming guidebook to bar-dining all over the city. Be sure you read this book with a glass of your favorite bubbly and a small plate close at hand. Cheers!

George Lang, Restaurateur/Owner
Café des Artistes

In *Belly Up to the Bar,* J. S. Mitchell teaches you how to experience the NY restaurant dining scene . . . via the bar. It's a unique and fun perspective, full of detail and vivid anecdotes of Mitchell's dining adventures. A great addition to any restaurant lover's library.

Eric Ripert, Executive Chef/Co-owner
Le Bernardin (Michelin ★★★)

Belly Up to the Bar

Dining with New York City's Celebrity Chefs without Reservation(s)

J. S. Mitchell

Cumberland House
Nashville, Tennessee

Belly Up to the Bar
Published by Cumberland House Publishing
431 Harding Industrial Drive
Nashville, Tennessee 37211

Cover design: James Duncan Creative
Book design: Mary Sanford

Photo credits: 11, Gina Jessica Smith; 26, Vivienne Hee; 119, Shimon & Tammar Photography; 167, Frances Janisch; 213, Robert Polidori

Library of Congress Cataloging-in-Publication Data

Mitchell, J. S.

Belly up to the bar : dining with New York City's celebrity chefs without reservation(s) / J.S. Mitchell.

p. cm.

Includes index.

ISBN-13: 978-1-58182-636-4 (pbk. : alk. paper)

ISBN-10: 1-58182-636-2 (pbk. : alk. paper)

1. Restaurants—New York (State)—New York—Guidebooks. 2. Bars (Drinking establishments)—New York (State)—New York—Guidebooks. I. Title.

TX907.3.N72N4584 2008
647.95747—dc22

2008080036

Printed in Canada
1 2 3 4 5 6 7—14 13 12 11 10 09 08

For Nikau Mitchell Tei,
my New Zealand grandson.
With hope that you will grow up
to enjoy one of life's great pleasures
of savoring the finest of foods in season
in the best of company for all seasons.

CONTENTS

THE RESTAURANTS

ACKNOWLEDGMENTS

The primary sources for this book are the top-rated restaurants that serve the full menu at the bar without reservations in the Big Apple—New York City, from South Seaport at the southern tip of Manhattan up through the financial district to Soho, the Village, to midtown and encompassing the Upper West and East Sides of this city. The best restaurants in the world were observed and studied, providing a vew of their magnificent tastes from on high, dining up at the bar. I am indebted to the publishers of the two sources used for the ratings of the restaurants: *Zagat 2008* and *Michelin 2008.*

I owe special thanks to the bartenders who are a font of information in their outgoing, friendly manner, always on their toes anticipating the needs of their patrons, and describing the drinks and menus from their special domain—that enclosed space behind their bar.

It's a pleasure to thank the bar diners whom I met along the way for conversation, sharing tastes, observations, and opinions. I am especially grateful for bar-dining friends who joined me often for dining adventures all over the city; especially Helen Chapman, Kate Daloz, Eric Kaplan, Jeff Kerney, and Lita Semerad.

I am eager to thank Ron Pitkin, publisher of Cumberland House, for his enthusiasm for *Belly Up to the Bar* and his commitment to an incredibly wide range of books that only a voracious reader could appreciate. Particular thanks, too, to editor Mary Sanford, who has my appreciation for a job smoothly and accurately well done.

And thanks go to the chefs who easily win my admiration for their hard work and creativity to distinguish themselves in this competitive field to earn top ratings. These celebrity chefs have an eye to give us the best in preparation and presentation in an ambience that suits our mood.

J. S. Mitchell
New York City
March 2008

INTRODUCTION

Dining alone tonight? No reservations, but you're in the mood for the excitement of a top-rated New York restaurant? There's a month of Saturday-night waits at Jean Georges? Wish you were tasting Gotham Bar and Grill's appetizer and dessert along with a great wine? Want camaraderie at the best place for Mexican? Seafood? French? Wish you were at Balthazar or Casa Mono or Lupa with the noisiest crowd and best food? Do you crave personal attention? Need the comfort of a Union Square Café bartender who will graciously whisk out a white linen napkin for your place setting at the bar as soon as you say, "Dining at the bar tonight . . ."? Want to call a friend at the last minute with a promise of dinner in Chelsea—to share the best steak in town at Craftsteak? Or in Murray Hill's Artisanal for the top cheese dishes, where everyone at the twelve-seat bar is having dinner? Or the organic farm-to-table at Blue Hill in the Village? You want the good stuff—light, sophisticated food after Lincoln Center at Picholine—without the formal restaurant scene? Then this is the book for you!

Dining bars are for New Yorkers what the pubs in England are for the villagers. Dining bars are found in Manhattan's best and most varied restaurants in the world. Dana, the bartender-

The bar at Picholine.

actor at Payard Bistro, replied to my dining at the bar query with, "Once they try the bar, they never go back to those stuffy little tables!" Dining at the bar has come of age. This dining in NYC's top-rated (Zagat and Michelin) restaurants phenomenon is taking the city by storm. What's "in" is that the very best—Le Bernardin, Kuruma Zushi, Modern Bar (at MoMA), Le Cirque, Babbo, wd-50, and the highest Michelin-starred chef in the world, Alain Ducasse, at Adour at Midtown's St. Regis Hotel—the top food and fashion trendsetters in town have designed their restaurants to welcome singles and doubles to dine as well as to drink at the bar. Come see and taste for yourself!

HOW TO USE THIS BOOK

Belly Up to the Bar is arranged alphabetically by restaurant. With a few exceptions, only restaurants serving the celebrity chef's full menu at the bar, and with a Zagat rating of 23 out of a possible 28, were included. Each of the restaurants was visited and revisited by the author. The 101 restaurant entries describe what it's like to dine at the bar, beginning with the place settings, which vary from formal white linen to the bare bar. Demographics follow: the number of bar seats, the number of people who are usually having a full meal, or dessert and champagne, or a drink and appetizer kind of service, and the bartender's information on the number of regulars dining at his bar. Age, gender, formality, dress, appearance of the crowd, and noise level are noted. Variety and price of beers and wines by the glass begin the bar's offerings.

All of the restaurants are expensive. *Belly Up to the Bar* describes only the best. Price is not the issue at the bar, however, because unlike the supercilious waiter who may act offended if patrons order fewer than three or four formal courses, the bartender is happy to serve an appetizer or dessert with your drink; or at Café des Artistes, for example, you may be there simply to enjoy a biscotti with a dessert wine. The food description is followed by the ambience of the bar scene. Are people talking to one another, or is the bartender the only direction for conversation? Are the bar diners sharing their food? How about those strangers sharing a taste of their neighbor's lobster risotto or cranberry bread pudding?

Belly Up to the Bar includes indexes by location, types of cuisine, and Michelin-star ratings. Search for what pleases you . . . and don't forget to try something new!

For an interactive online map of the restaurants in this book, please go to www.cumberlandhouse.com/bellyuptothebar

ALIAS

76 Clinton Street (Rivington Street) *Zagat: 23*
212-505-5011 *www.aliasrestaurant.com*
Chef: Anthony Rose

Let's start right off with a funky storefront restaurant on the Lower East Side to warm you up to the idea of top food at the bar. Don't let the bodega look on the outside scare you off, because when you step inside this small room, you'll smile at the contrasting modern room with colorful decor and bar. The very friendly staff all come together with weekend brunches and a Sunday supper three-course special for $25 to make it a neighborhood favorite. Neighborhood favorites are always interesting to try out, as you see the people who have learned what's good from among a lot of choices. Many would agree that Clinton Street and the Lower East Side is a resurrected food favorite for all those who know New York. Not to mention that you won't find better food and drink for the money in all of Manhattan!

Checking out the five-beer list will give you an idea of their creativity: one from Mexico, another from Belgium, and then three micros from New York, Maine, and Vermont. As I hadn't tried the Hennepin Farmhouse Ale before, that was my $6 choice (the Corona and Stella were $5). The two cocktail house favorites are a white wine fresh-fruit sangria by the glass, half liter, or full carafe. And the house margarita on the rocks for $6. Classic cocktails are also available, including a ginger martini for $10, and a Dark and Stormy—dark rum with ginger beer and fresh lime, for $8.

A starter to share sounded wonderful, a taco plate with one of shrimp; one of duck confit with wild rice, chestnuts, and cherry sauce; and the third of roasted mushroom with cucumber and sour cream. The entrées included two fish dishes and one vegetarian, which was a braised Spanish onion stuffed with spring vegetables, ramps, peas, asparagus, grilled leeks, and a red pepper almond sauce. Doesn't that sound tempting? The meat choices are pork, chicken, and two beef selections.

Special occasions, such as the monthly "Full Moon Menu," make Alias a fun place to go, and of course if you take someone to the five-seat bar, you can taste more. There are usually five desserts offered to include chocolate, an apple tart, an ice-cream sundae, and a mini ice-cream sandwich. Give it a try . . . I've been twice, once to ask directions and I stayed because it was so charming, and the second time I brought a convert.

ALLEN & DELANCEY

115 Allen Street (Delancey Street) | *Zagat: Not yet*
212-253-5400 | *www.allen&delancey.net*
Chef: Neil Ferguson

Lower East Side . . . the au currant restaurant location for big-time newcomers with their big-time innovative creations in food, mood, and interiors. Celebrity chef Neil Ferguson left the UK with a Michelin-starred record last year for a midtown experience, until he and his too-bossy boss parted ways and he decided it was time for his own shop. And wait until you are sitting at the bar in this fabulous shop!

The first of three candlelit rooms with exposed brick walls is the bar room. With a ceiling of two-by-fours and printed tin and wooden floors, the bar takes the whole room, and all twelve seats were taken by diners and others waiting for a seat at 8:45 p.m. on a Saturday night in January. This warm cozy bar has a Village '50s feel with the antiques and oil paintings and the feel of a literary club or UK university rooms instead of a New York City restaurant.

There couldn't have been more than two people at the bar over forty, and I was one of them. A very thirtysomething crowd, and this was one of the few places with as many if not more women at the bar than men. Gay and straight couples, as well as singles at the bar, and mainly couples in the other two dining rooms, with a few over fifty. The comfort zone would include anyone, however, as it's a relaxed place with a nice Saturday night buzz, and you don't have to shout to be heard by the person next to you.

The menu, the menu! I've seldom seen a better beer list, and when I decided on the Dog Fish Head IPA, my choices were a 60-, 90-, or 120-minute size! I went for the 60. The beer buyer came over after I remarked about the list, and I learned that he has only local microbrews on his list, his criteria being that he can drive to the brewery in one day. As he has two Northern Vermont beers on his list (Magic Hat and Otter Creek), I realized he included a seven-hour drive in his one-day rule . . . but hey, he has the best beer list! There were five white and four red wines by the glass and three bubblies. Many orders of the Delancey cocktail—a splash of pomegranate juice with champagne—were flying out of the bar. A white linen triangle was placed in front of me along with two breads: a small baguette and a soft herbed roll. Allen & Delancey are prideful about their sweet butter. I started with the signature starter, caramelized bone marrow with caviar, as I had only had bone marrow ensconced in the bone! The menu of eight appetizer choices and seven entrée selections makes it seem even more like a club than a public dining room, adding to the relaxed, familiar ambiance. Mark, the man on my left (who knows bars, as he used to work at Union Square Café), had ordered the leeks vinaigrette, truffled fingerlings, and prosciutto shavings, which he said held up to its promise.

After studying the seven entrées—three were fish—I chose the braised fluke with cauliflower cream, parsley root, and trompettes, and it was simply exquisite! Fresh fish, lightly braised, topped the parsley root that were as big as broccoli stems, a few slices of mushrooms—perfecto! The British chef serves horseradish with the sirloin steak, but it was the very interesting lamb plate, which Mark ordered, that stole my vote. It was a loin chop and a braised middle neck on a potato purée. The purée was indeed purée—it could have been called "prideful butter with a splash of potato"! A taste of Mark's middle neck lamb reminded me of a New Zealand umu I had just been to where the lamb is cooked in the ground under palm leaves against hot stones for hours. And it reminded me, too, of my spring lamb stew recipe made with lamb neck, which is so sweet and tender. You won't want to miss out on dining at this very friendly vintage Village bar in the Lower East Side. The first room is designed just for us . . . very happy bar diners with a room of our own without reservations.

ALTO

11 East 53rd Street (5th and Madison Avenues) *Zagat: 26*
212-308-1099 *www.altorestaurant.com*
Closed: Sundays *Chef: Michael White*

If you can't get into this big-time Madison–Fifth Avenue top-rated formal Italian restaurant after a visit to MoMA or your midtown meeting, there are six seats in the cool setting of a black bar on a gray slate floor in the anteroom between the glass door and the restaurant, where the coat check and the reservation desk are located. Even though the bar is not within the dining room and you won't smell or see the restaurant scene, you can still go with a pal to get celebrity chef Michael White's full menu and taste some of the best Italian in town.

At 7:30 p.m. on a Saturday night, everyone at the bar was there for a drink while waiting for their table, which they had reserved weeks ahead. But wait! Let's say you are in town for one night and dying to taste White's renowned northern Italian–Austrian specialty of herbed spaetzle with slow-braised rabbit, caramelized parsnips, mint, and parmigiana. Why settle for less when you can profit from this opportunity? With no reservations in sight no matter who you know, belly up to the bar, keeping company with the sippers, and know that a single doesn't usually wait too long at the carefully guarded reservation system for a seat at the bar. Ask for the extensive (twelve thousand bottles) wine list to entertain you while waiting for a seat at the bar.

Even though food critics have suggested that if dining at Alto one should focus on the dumplings, a specialty of the region from which Alto was named, I didn't feel like pot stickers filled with Swiss chard. Instead, I went for the poached Malpeque oysters with cauliflower soup, crisp shallots with capers, and a glass of white to go with it. As Alto is very well known for its wine list, I decided to take the recommendation of the sommelier rather than my usual New Zealand sauvignon blanc, and instead tried the Elena Walch Gewürztraminer at $16 because it comes from northern Italy, the region of Alto's inspiration. My friend Chris, who joined me this evening for a special treat on a weeknight, wanted to try the highly recommended pastas, so he chose the braised oxtail cappellacci with a parmigiana broth and horseradish. He ordered an Italian Foradori Teroldego red at $18 to go with the game dish he intended to try for the entrée. Even though I don't usually overdo the carbs, I didn't want to leave without sharing a taste of the polenta, a miracle of this chef, which has a whisper of vanilla with truffles folded in at the last minute. In order to try an entrée in addition to the first and pasta courses, we decided to share the venison. (That's the beauty of dining at the bar . . . sharing an entrée is an every-evening occurrence!) It was a seared loin of venison that came with chestnut polenta, so voilà—the polenta course.

No room for dessert, although their dessert wines were a temptation that we could not resist when offered a glass of Abbazia di Novacella from the restaurant's Alto-Adige region. The evening ended with this sublime wine and one bite of the chef's biscotti. The food transported us, so if you don't mind the "entryway" ambience, you'll love the food experience.

ANNISA

13 Barrow Street
(7th Avenue South and West 4th Street) *Zagat: 27; Michelin:* ★
212-741-6699 *www.annisarestaurant.com*
Chef: Anita Lo

Calm, très, très elegant, white, tiny, sophisticated Asian-feeling space with five bar seats. *Annisa* is the Arabic word for "women." And now just imagine a perfect, Parisian beer glass instead of the usual "too big for anyone's sensibilities" beer tumbler or mug. Not only that, all you beer devotees, but there are three draft beers, and the bartender is happy to give you a taste before you choose.

White linen triangles are placed on the bar for the diners, and water without asking. There was one couple at the bar, two single men, and one woman, all in different stages of dinner. There are nine wine selections by the glass from $9 to $18. Women, take note: The ninety wine labels carried by Annisa are all made by women winemakers or companies owned by women from all over the globe. Several champagne-based cocktails are served at the bar. The appetizers range from $13 to $18, the entrées from $28 to $32. The man next to me was enjoying a spicy grilled eggplant and lentils soup with yogurt. I considered the white tuna tartare with Korean chili but decided instead on a Shanghai-style seared foie gras soup dumplings with jicama. With what? Who ever heard of jicama (a tuber vegetable)? Most of us will find many unfamiliar ingredients on the menu. The bartender seemed pleased that we asked for a description of the obscure. While waiting for their entrées, the couple on my right were enjoying the bar snack of a Chinese salted egg, which they said was an interesting first for them.

Studying the menu, my bar-dining pal Helen and I noted that there were four fish selections, a rack of lamb, and a pot-au-feu, all of which appeared to be enjoyed by the diners in the upper-level dining room as I watched them leave the restaurant with looks of pure satisfaction on their faces. Beer and foie gras soup with dumplings had to be followed by a dessert for me that evening. The pumpkin pudding with wafer and ginger ice cream was my pick without a spoon of disappointment. A top espresso fulfilled all expectations at this highly rated (with reason) restaurant. Interested in some of the most creatively prepared fusion food in the city in the loveliest of settings? Take a seat without reservation(s) at Annisa for a Michelin-star experience.

Women over forty . . . please take note! How many times have I heard, "I wouldn't sit at a bar!" Thinking sports bar, burgers and beer, guys hitting on you, right? Not proper! Here's the place to begin. Remember, we are talking top-of-the-line—the best-rated food in all the world! Everyone who goes to these restaurants is looking for great eating experiences. Start here, go to any of Danny Meyer's restaurants, and by the third bar, I'll bet you'll be hooked. Not only that—when you have a late business meeting, your husband or best friend is out of town and you want to have a special dinner, or just for a festive evening, hop on the #6 train and be just half a block from Tamarind, a top Indian restaurant, or walk across Spring Street to Aquagrill for a warm welcome by the bartender, even on your first visit. Or stay on the Upper East Side and walk over to Payard. Be brave, enjoy life with the rest of us on the spur of the moment without reservation(s)!

AQUAGRILL

210 Spring Street (6th Avenue)
212-274-0505

Zagat: 26
www.aquagrill.com
Chef: Jeremy Marshall

Twenty-six oyster choices from as far away as the Coromandel Peninsula in New Zealand and as close as Wellfleet, Massachusetts, are available for diners at the bar. All twelve bar seats were occupied on a Monday night in May at 8:00 p.m. And no wonder! The professional bartender, Jai, knows his oysters, knows his menu and food preparations, and knows his charm! Oh boy, this is the place to be when it comes to fish with a touch of Asian for the tried-and-true. And you can even order one oyster! You don't have to do the usual "six minimum."

If you are late, take the Sixth Avenue subway to Spring Street and you will be a half block away. But if you are by yourself tonight, or want to slow down a bit after your fast day, take the #6 to Spring and walk across, past Balthazar, enjoying the few fascinating blocks and life on Spring Street until you get to 210. We waited about ten minutes for two bar seats together, and if we had been solo, there would have been no wait.

Lamps and photo frames of seashells are the decor; a wooden bar adds to the warmth and comfort of the dining experience; and everyone likes a footrest, especially like this one, more a shelf than a rail, which means we can put our stuff there! The six whites and six reds by the glass range from $8 to $16. There are four beers on tap including a Guinness Smithwick's Ale, which has to be my all-time favorite find in the past year, and the three old standby bottles—you know them, I don't have to spell out Bud, Heineken, and Amstel Light, do I? The Smithwick's does excuse those ordinary labels, don't you agree?

Easy to forgive the bottle selections when the chef sent out an amuse-bouche: a potato chip cradling a strip of avocado with chopped raw fish. A tasty mouthful to whet the anticipating nerve endings! Bar dining pal Lita and I started with three oysters each with our beer. The oysters were not exactly what I was looking for, however, and so Jai added another to see if that was the briny taste I had in mind. Of course it was.

Michael, the young bond salesman on my left, was having

the signature dish, salmon-crusted falafel with soy and ginger, following his starter of tuna-belly tartare, which of course he shared with this diner and her bar-dining friend. We had a first-time entrée, a New Zealand orange roughy, whitefish, sweet, flaked to perfection with ranks (the buzzword in the top kitchens on spring menus), and an asparagus sauce over a thin cushion of polenta. Superb. Only from a 26-rated kitchen!

I had a New Zealand sauvignon blanc for $9.50, and Lita a California pinot noir for $13. A discussion of a James Bond's favorite cocktail came up as the diners on my right and left exchanged preferences of a Vesper, which is a martini spin-off of one-third vodka and two-thirds gin, with a thin layer of Lilay on top. Michael informed us that the name comes from James Bond's girlfriend, Vesper Lynn, which is all in the book, and she always ordered it in a goblet. He decided to try it with half vodka and half gin in a large martini glass—goblet size. As the two Vespers went back and forth between them, I was requested to take a taste on the way, so it became a very festive evening, which evidently is typical at Aquagrill. We topped it all off with a mocha crème brûlée with two thin hazelnut strips on the side, and a plate of cookies from the chef. Excellent espresso ended our evening. Well, after bidding good night to bartender Jai and James Bond expert Michael, of course!

AQUAVIT

65 East 55th Street (Madison and Park Avenues) *Zagat: 25*
212-307-7311 *www.aquavit.org*
Chefs: Marcus Samuelsson and Johan Svensson

How many Scandinavian restaurants are there in NYC? Go ahead . . . take a guess. Right you are! Aquavit is the only big-time Scandinavian, even though chef-owner Marcus Samuelsson has a lunch restaurant (AQ), and there is a small chain (three) of smorgasbord and Swedish meatball variety. Head for the bar and thirteen bar seats in the front café of this highly rated, minimalist, cool-look restaurant. Don't worry about feeling cold, however, even at the modernist-designed gray slate bar, because "Aquavit" is the name of the Scandinavian liquor, and the signature cocktail, made on the premises to warm you up. Think Cosmopolitan at the bar of Jean Georges, think Aquapolitan at Aquavit. Here it is: starting with the homemade orange and lemon aquavits, add orange liquor, lemon and lime juices, and to warm up that color—cranberry juice. Or . . . if you want to go straight to the warm-up mode without waiting for the mixing of all that nonalcoholic citrus, have the Horseradish Aquavit. That will surely do it! Aquavit is proud of their own White Cranberry Aquavit, which they spent several years developing and which is now imported and can be ordered online. If you aren't up to the Aquapolitan or Horseradish Aquavit, there is a wine list with six international whites, reds, and dessert choices by the glass, and seven beers including two from Denmark and Germany, an IPA from Brooklyn, and I chose the Whale's Tale Pale Ale to keep in character of Scandinavian fish.

Dining. Oh, yes, we are here for a 25 rating of top Scandinavian cuisine! Did I mention that this Scandinavian chef grew up in Sweden but was born in Ethiopia? He loves creating tastes from the two cultures, and that's exactly what his food is about. For example, how often do you think you could get salsify noodles in a saffron-coconut broth if you were in Stockholm? There is a pretheater prix-fixe, three-course menu for $55 before 6:15 that includes the signature herring sampler, and you can try the chocolate truffle cream that is prepared with sweet milk, corn, and served with lemon sorbet. How many times have you tried that combination? The prix-fixe dinner menu of three courses is $82, and when I was there I started with the yellowtail, duck tongue, sea urchin, and lime, simply because I don't believe I had tasted duck tongue before. I have to admit, though, that by the time I had my first Aquavit, my mind wasn't exactly on the subtleties of duck tongue. The yellowtail was followed by the poached black sea bass with eggplant, soy beans, and citrus. I thought this plate was our Swedish-Ethiopian chef at his best. Give it a try for yourself; it's something new. (If you check the website before you go, notice that it is a "dot org" address, not the usual "dot com," . . . speaking from experience.)

ARTISANAL

2 Park Avenue
(Enter on 32nd Street; Madison and Park Avenues) *Zagat: 23*
212-725-8585 *www.artisinalbistro.com*
Chef: Terrance Brennan

Okay, you cheese-loving bar diners—come on over to a thriving French brasserie and choose one of the twelve bar seats or another twelve unreserved seats in the lounge. But wait! You'll think you have walked into Balthazar by mistake, but you haven't. It's a wonderful high-ceilinged, red (well, burgundy-colored) banquettes and walls, French lamps, a very French kind of place. Or you will think you've hit a Parisian fromagerie when you get your first whiff of cheese walking through the door. In fact, we are talking a menu of 250 types of cheese, with a retail counter at which you may purchase or send some of these world-class cheeses.

Colleague Latin teacher Jeff and I got one of those coveted bar seats because Jeff went early (6:30) to make sure, and he had chosen a plate of three cheeses for a starter. For an entrée, Jeff thought only steak-frites would do in such a French ambience, and I can never resist sautéed skate wing whenever I see it on the menu. We noticed that the prix-fixe menu, a great choice for some other time, started with soup or salad or mussels, offered an asparagus risotto or prime hanger steak for the next course, and ended with a cheesecake, or selection of cheeses, or warm chocolate soufflé cake for $35. We went for the famous tarte tatin because we had heard about it from a teaching pal at school—it is cooked with just a tad of cheddar baked into the crust. Oh, boy . . . savor that espresso and look around at the happy faces of the people dining at the bar.

I returned a month later on a Monday night at 10 p.m. to check out the bar-dining crowd one more time, and even then every seat was taken. I had just checked three other highly rated restaurants and found few of the dinner crowd at the bar at that hour. A thirties-to-sixties group sat at the bar, almost all of them dining. Artisanal was jumping and funning and eating cheese. What a way to live!

A VOCE

41 Madison Avenue (26th Street)
212-545-8555

Zagat: 25; Michelin: ★
www.avocerestaurant.com
Chef: Andrew Carmellini

Duck meatball antipasto (duck, veal, and a dash of foie gras in the center) with dried cherry mostarda. Tripe with a fried duck egg. Grandma's ravioli and a sea bass in a basil broth served with a few clams, scallops, and shrimp. These are just a few of this chef's creative top-of-the-line dishes. With eight seats at the bar, friendly bartender Paul has been at A Voce since it opened at Madison Square Park a year ago; waiters visit with the bar diners as they pick up their drinks or with suggestions from the menu. A mix of ages and formality make for a very comfortable environment, no matter which you prefer. At the tables with brown leather swivel chairs, two couples with men in shirtsleeves drinking their beer from the bottle were next to two men in business suits. A few tables of businessmen—six at one of them; the rest of the tables with couples of all ages. At the bar were one couple and two solo women dining, while the others were enjoying a martini while they waited for their dining partner to show up.

A modern look with red walls, black metallic hangings, and magnificent floral displays, high energy within a large, uncrowded space was the ambience. In the middle of dinner on this Monday evening at 8 p.m., in swept THE celebrity chef Jean-Georges, "who often eats here," according to bartender Paul.

As soon as I asked for a menu, a mesh place mat of black and gray squares was placed before me, ice water, white linen napkin, and dinnerware, and soon a tray of thickly sliced crusty Italian bread appeared and a white ceramic dish of olive oil with a drop of balsamic vinegar on top. Starting right off with an interesting wine list, glasses ranging from $7 to $15; the beer list was much more interesting than the usual Italian Moretti and Peroni beers to include a California IPA (India pale ale), which was just right with the duck meatballs, although it was fun to see a Belgium beer, La Chouffe, for $27. Yes, it was a large bottle, 750 cl, but still, amusing to see the beer a higher price than any of the wines by the glass. With beer in hand, I studied the menu, deciding between an appetizer and dessert or an entrée such as the lamb tortellini with escarole, grapes, and Piave cheese; or the braised veal soffritto with Andrew Carmellini's polenta, which I had heard is out of this world. The signature dish of duck meatballs won out.

Lucky for me, the thirtysomething businesswoman just in from L.A. moved over when the martini men left, so that I could see and, as it turned out, taste the sea bass in the basil broth that she ordered, and share my dessert of very thin phyllo-encased baked apple slices, topped with a dollop of sorbet. Like many businesspeople from out of town, she followed NYC's celebrity chefs and knew when they came west to open top restaurants in L.A. She always dines at the bar because, in her experience, "it's difficult for a single woman to get a decent situated table at the top places. But up here, I can check it all out and enjoy myself." I suggested that when she calls she make the reservation for Mr. So-and-so, and she quickly agreed that she would prefer to be at the bar anyway, where it is less formal and much friendlier.

The menu, printed daily and changed often, is not overwhelming with choices, although a great variety of fish, veal, and lamb is always a possibility. Likewise, maybe five desserts plus the sorbets and cheese selections. Almost always on the menu are Tuscan doughnuts with chocolate sauce, a panna cotta, and a fruit dessert. If the time and weather are in your favor, take a look at Madison Square Park on your way in . . . established in 1870, and a delightful NYC public space.

BABBO

110 Waverly Place
(MacDougal Street and 6th Avenue)
212-777-0303

Zagat: 27; Michelin: ★
www.babbonyc.com
Chef: Mario Batali

We had to wait patiently as celebrity chef-owner Mario Batali was having a serious wine discussion with two of the ten guests at the bar. Babbo was bursting with energy, upstairs and down, all ages with many of the forties and fifties-plus upstairs in a major skylighted space, with a most striking Victorian carpeting on the stairs to the second floor. The wine director, whom Helen and I had met at the Eleven Madison bar a few nights ago, was everywhere: at the table giving suggestions, at the bar conferring with the waiters, and at the entrance discoursing on the wine list.

A few waited for tables at 7:30 p.m., and by 8:35 the bar was five-deep in eager customers. Mostly couples were eating at the bar, and one single traveling businessman from Washington, DC, on my right, who returned for a second night after being so happy at his new find, which he had discovered on his own because he couldn't get reservations anywhere he wanted to go. Now he can't wait to tell his friends about eating at NYC's best restaurants at the bar. He shared all of his selections.

There were six beers to choose from, draughts and bottles, and I ordered the Italian beer because of its origin, not its flavor. Bowls of tiny olives were on the bar, and a sizable list of wines by the glass from $9. Babbo is known for its exceptional Italian wine list, and I have heard people being advised to be sure to bring a copy of their credit rating for the top reds, which can go as high as $650 a bottle. It was hard to choose an entrée among the many unusual choices that included ravioli filled with beef cheeks, ravioli filled with quail liver with a butter and sage sauce, pumpkin polenta, snapper tartare, sweetbreads, calamari, and octopus. I gave some thought to the rock shrimp with New Zealand mussels in a broth with peppers, which Helen ordered, and I then decided on the ravioli with beef cheeks and shiitake mushrooms, which were exquisite. Excellent bread was served by a waiter from the dining room.

The bartenders were asked a million questions about the menu and were trained well to explain the fine points of food preparation as well as the wine selections. Wines and martinis are the drinks of choice from this bar. The rack of lamb appeared to be the favored meat for the evening, although after a taste, shared by Ed, the DC neighbor on my right, I was pleased to have gone for the unusual. For dessert, the bartender recommended the spuma di ricotta with pomegranate, and we chose the spiced chestnut saffiosu with roasted pears, crème fraîche, and pear sorbetto (all desserts were $11). We could have had a soup and sorbetto, or sciffron panna cotta with blood oranges. The dessert was very good, but it didn't nearly reach the excellence of the entrée. Next time I'll listen to the bartender!

Returning on a Thursday evening in June, as is often the case a single seat was easy, although there were waits for the doubles. I sat beside a woman who lives nearby and who eats regularly at Babbo. She said that the spaghetti with clam sauce is one of the best, but as I had never tried the ravioli stuffed with goose liver with a balsamic sauce, I thought that would be the experience of the evening. Experience it was! Much too thick and scalding hot—burn-the-roof-of-your-mouth hot, I mean—heavy, and too much of it for a June night. Christine (the bar diner on my right) runs a business at home all day and eats out within walking distance of Washington Square to Union Square almost every night. In fact when we were talking about eating at the bar and I mentioned the hook under the bar to put one's things, she told me that the hook was the idea of a waitress named Carolyn at the Union Square Café. Carolyn is the one who told Danny Meyer that women who dine at the bar need a hook to put their purse or shopping bag or briefcase on, and from ever after, all of his restaurants have that convenient hook. Well done, Carolyn! Oh, yes, back to Babbo . . . if you are after the Italian menu, and a lively five-deep-at-the-bar scene, then Babbo is the place for you. Order the spaghetti with clam sauce!

BALTHAZAR

80 Spring Street (Lexington Avenue) *Zagat: 23*
212-965-1414 *www.balthazarny.com*
Chef: Keith McNally

Looking for a New York crowd in a Parisian setting? Then Balthazar will not disappoint! They say that the Balthazar setting was moved from Paris mirror by mirror, chandelier by chandelier, complete with red leather banquettes in a warehouse space and a constant parade of celebs, debs, and out-of-town businesspeople. At 8:30 p.m. on a Monday evening in the springtime, no one was having dinner at the bar, and many more men than women were having their after-work drink. A thirties and forties crowd, several men stood around each bar seat at the zinc. Remember, Americans, that *zinc* is the French term for "bar" because in Paris all of the bars were covered with zinc until WWII when it was scrapped for the war effort, although the name continues without the actual zinc. Many establishments in Paris have returned to zinc bars as part of a Parisian 1920s and 1930s look. By 10:30 p.m., half the bar seats were taken by diners (or the same men started getting hungry). The maître d' said that as many women dine regularly at the bar as men, so if you see that when you are there, be sure to send me an e-mail with your count (BellyUpToBarNYC@aol.com)!

The late-night crowd soon learns that Balthazar has a late supper menu—just like Paris—that includes eggs and boudin noir. Ambience is everything at Balthazar. It is very entertaining to watch the restaurant action reflected in the mirror as you sit at the bar, or watch directly if you sit at the end of the bar. It's a fashion show par excellence with a lot of cool strutters taking the walk. I was sitting between an out-of-town L.A. space-ads guy and an Englishman from a local publishing house. Both had been to Balthazar before. Todd, from L.A., was eating from the raw bar and had ordered a variety of East Coast oysters, enjoying a microbrew ale with them. Keeping in the French mood of Balthazar, Jon was halfway through the steak-frites, especially interested in our American french fries. He had tasted three reds, which the bartender was happy to describe and pour for tasting. As busy and hectic as this bar is, it is not short on service or patience in describing any of the more than three hundred wines on the list. I tasted the french fries and agreed, they were as good as the best yet from MarkJoseph, the steak house in the financial district that of course knows how to crisp those fries! Enjoy the entertainment at Balthazar when you're in the mood for an American-in-nineteenth-century-Paris experience in bustling NYC!

BAR AMERICAIN

152 West 52nd Street (6th and 7th Avenues) *Zagat: 23*
212-265-9700 *www.baramericain.com*
Chef: Bobby Flay

A full, spacious overhanging balcony adds to the high energy on a winter Wednesday night at 8:30, and it sounded like all 275 seats in the restaurant were filled as well. Not one of the sixteen bar seats was open, and there were a few dining at the raw bar, but for the most part, it was all after-business talk in clusters around the bar. At least three-fourths of the seats were taken by men in their thirties to sixties, and more than half the dinner tables were filled by men. A midtown suits look, and the buzz of great global business being discussed.

Back again on a Monday night at 7 p.m. and aha! A seat among the midtown group. It happens that one guy was buying for his colleagues, and everyone around me was eating shrimp-tomatillo, crab-coconut cocktail, or raw oysters and clams. Enjoying beer or martinis, the talk was of closing a deal that had been iffy from the start. A very festive evening at the bar. When a suited woman came along and sat on my right, I was happy to have an informant who often comes into Bar Americain after her office closes around 7 p.m. She said that in her publishing house office, the lamb sausage with white beans and sauced with a red zinfandel is very popular as everyone is starved right after work. She ordered her favorite, though, a grilled pizza topped with smoked trout and salmon and herbed with dill. Of course I got a bite or two and agreed, it was a great appetizer with a drink. I decided to go straight for the plate of the day, which on Monday was a roasted whole fish with crawfish sauce. Had I looked up the menu on the Web, I would have waited a night and tried the grilled sea scallops with white beans, apple cider, and sage. Margaret, the senior editor sitting next to me, agreed that the Bar Americain is a major fish, steak, and chops place and that the plate of the day is always a treat that you don't have to think about, just order Monday!

Looking around the restaurant and up at the balcony, it is easy to see that every table fills up fast and by 8 p.m. Americain was almost at full force. The drinkers were leaving their workday, and the diners were on their way to dinner in this formal-looking restaurant with an informal feeling.

BELLAVITAE

24 Minetta Lane (McDougal Street and 6th Avenue) *Zagat: 22*
212-473-5121 *www.bellavitae.com*
Chef: Amy Teichman

Head straight to the back of this charming Italian trattoria to the nine-seat dining bar, a semicircle of beautiful white Italian marble. You'll feel as if you are in your favorite, cozy Village club, even on your first visit. Better yet, take an out-of-towner to show off getting there in a secluded West Village lane, proving that NYC has everything from modern Chelsea steak houses to Bellavitae. With wood-beamed ceilings, a wood-burning oven, Fortuny lamps, and waitstaff as warm and welcoming as the decor, you will not be disappointed.

Start with one of the Italian-only beers or wine, and you can test the chef with his olive oil–fried meatballs or the stuffed peppers with Sicilian tuna and capers. The appetizers are small plates, followed by four pastas and four meat dishes on the menu. Sitting beside a regular who lives in the Village, Alphonso, who is from an Italian family and knows what to order as he eats out most evenings, I got to taste the meatballs, which were a treat. The *New York Times* had just described a variety of meatball recipes from the celebrity chefs in a major piece in the Dining Out section. This one was prepared with veal, pork, and herbs, and was just the combination that satisfies the traditional anticipation in Italian meatballs.

With an Italian friend from out of town, we headed for Bellevitae in the West Village. Small plates are the way to go to taste the chef. We ordered glasses of an Italian red and a white, and four small plates rather than an entrée, starting with a black and green olive paté with chopped egg and anchovy for $9, followed by beets roasted in the brick oven with agrumato oranges, pecorino, and extra-virgin olive oil. Spaghetti with fulvi, pecorino, rosemary, and cracked black pepper for $15. Coming from an old Italian family in Barre, Vermont, where the granite stonecutters came straight from Italy, Fosco couldn't believe his comfort level at a New York City Italian restaurant. Of course, dining at the bar is always more informal and friendlier, but still, it was the menu, the smell, and the creativity of the Italian standards that he raved about. No doubt about it, finding this West Village bar was the major event of his trip to New York City.

BEPPE

42 East 22nd Street (Park Avenue South and Broadway) *Zagat: 23*
212-982-8422 *www.beppenyc.com*
Closed: Sundays *Chef: Marc Taxiera*

A long, narrow passageway to the restaurant is always full, with eight seats at the bar and two more at the window. The atmosphere is informal and feels like a neighborhood place, even on the first visit from another neighborhood. All ages were dining at the bar, although there were more men than women, and conversation was the sound, rather than music or major voice noises. This is a restaurant with its own farm in upstate New York—the menu follows the seasons from its organically grown produce—and a hog farm, which translates into the Beppe's own sausages, salami, and house-made prosciutto. An old and rustic Tuscan look of wooden floors, exposed brick walls, and open-beam ceilings adds to the warmth of this restaurant, as does the working fireplace in the dining room.

Marc's menu matches the decor, as Tuscany is his palette and imagination starts in his taste buds. The olive oil is from Tuscany, the sea salt from the Mediterranean, the greens all fresh from the green market. I had been told to try anything that said *farro* while at Beppe's. I also knew ahead of time that the cannoli at Beppe's isn't the soggy solid dough that is common in Italian bakeries, but rather a rolled lace cookie filled with a sugar cream. Listening to the advice of others, I spotted farrotto on the menu, a risotto-style nutty grain with seasonal vegetables. As it was the fall season, I was in luck with parsnips, turnips, a bit of squash, and beautifully roasted beets. As I expected, all the wines (except for French champagne) are from Italy, and several by the glass in red, rosé, and white. I had only two beers to choose from—you guessed it, Peroni or Moretti. I always ask for the darker one, taking the lesser of the two evils (when I really longed for a Vermont Wolover IPA). Oh well, don't we all know that eating and drinking the same tastes weakens the taste buds, our discernment of flavors, and smells? Of course we know that! It's good to keep changing, trying new tastes, textures, and colors in order to assure ourselves that we actually like what we think we like.

The man on my left told me that he eats at a bar at least four nights a week, and one of those nights is always Beppe's, within walking distance of his job. He was in the middle of the Milanese, a pan-fried pork chop topped with marinated radishes and arugala. He doesn't have a "usual" order, as the chef changes the menu regularly, and he likes to try whatever new dish the chef is presenting. After eating the filling risotto, and planning to take the #6 train home rather than walk to the Upper East Side, I decided to skip the secondi and go straight for the sweet cannoli. A bittersweet digestive (this is Tuscany territory, after all!), Nocino, was the perfect ending to a friendly, informal, very comfortable top-dining experience at celebrity chef Marc Taxiera's place.

BLT FISH

21 West 17th Street (5th and 6th Avenues) *Zagat: 23*
212-691-8888 *www.bltfish.com*
Closed: Sundays *Chef: Laurent Tourondel*

A description of "raucous" would be an understatement for this lookalike Cape Cod fish shack. I noted booths along one wall, round tables each filled with five or six thirtysomethings to fiftysomethings, and a long wooden bar with twelve seats feeding mostly men and a few women. A TV showed a game while music blasted from someplace else, and the noise level of the oyster and mussel eaters rose to hit the Christmas lights lining the upper reaches of the moulding between walls and ceiling. A friendly place, black-and-white photos, and seafood junkies having fun come quickly to mind. A young British couple who had just arrived in NYC sat on my right eating oysters, muscles, fresh asparagus, and trying several of the draught beers. An L.A. Web-business guy stood on my left, meeting with his old college friend from New York City, who knows all the best NYC dining bars, were waiting for a table. His favorite place is BLT Fish; hers is dining at the bar at Babbo. Posted behind the bar on a black electric signboard are the types of beer, oysters, and most of the BLT Fish menu. Three draughts are offered: Brooklyn, Whale's Tale Pale Ale, and Blue Point. The ten bottles were unusually interesting; even though Budweiser topped the list, below were Anchor Steam, Coors Dark Brown, Fisherman's Brew, Hitachino Nest pale ale, Brooklyn Local and Abita Light. I thought the Whale's Tale Pale Ale was most appropriate and it turned out to be just the taste I had hoped for.

On the board were nine oysters from the East Coast: Prince Edward Island to Cape Cod, Long Island, farmed Belons from Maine, and the West Coast specials were from British Columbia, Oregon, and Washington, all priced from $1.85 apiece to $2.95. Paper place mats printed with instructions on how to crack a lobster, and a tea towel for a napkin were placed in front of the diners at the bar. Having read of their famous Maine lobster roll, I ordered it without question and after the first bite remembered why a Vermonter never eats lobster south of Boston—there was nothing New England about it because there were so many herbs mixed with so much mayo that there was no way to taste the lobster, even when trying hard. Texture and color were right, but obviously not going by the northern New England seafood rules ends up with disappointment.

When I go back—remember, ordering is everything at a restaurant—I will start with a cup of clam chowder, move on to the West Coast oysters, and maybe have a side of that wonderful-looking asparagus plate on my right. Everyone agreed that the fries and the cheese bread (herb and cheese in a croissant-type bread) that is served with every order is top of the line.

Because I was in the neighborhood, I couldn't resist stopping by Union Square Café for dessert and coffee where I could forget the mayo-herbed lobster roll and top off my evening with a new Union Square dessert offering of brown butter cake with whiskey pineapple, and vanilla ice cream, followed by a superb espresso. The woman in her forties on my left told me that next to Union Square Café, she loved to dine at Lupa best. Mickey, the friendly bartender of twelve years, announced to me that it was time to move on and that he is opening his own wine bar at 28 West Eighth Street, the 8th Street Winecellar. It was at the Union Square Café that I first got the idea of writing this book. It was Mickey who listened to the idea. I couldn't wait to tell him that my fieldwork was now completed; this was my last dessert and coffee to go into the manuscript. I started and ended with Mickey at Union Square Café. When my paid bill arrived, I learned that this last treat at the bar was on Mickey.

And now you know to go to BLT Fish for noisy fun, to Lupa for festive fun, and to Union Square Café to hear and be heard fun! And before we dine at the bar, let's give Mickey's new 8th Street Winecellar a try.

BLT PRIME

111 East 22nd Street
(Lexington Avenue and Park Avenue South) *Zagat: 24*
212-995-8500 *www.bltprime.com*
Chef: Laurent Tourondel

Party place! A dress-up party place. A young crowd having fun, noisy in an upbeat way. It's a loud, happy bar scene with men double and triples and a scattering of women sitting and standing at the bar, very much like The Modern. Be sure you let the bartender know as soon as you get there that you are waiting to belly up to the bar for dinner. The seats are always taken. Your fifteen-minute wait, however, isn't anything compared to waiting weeks for a table reservation. All of that happiness and people waiting for their tables raise the conversation level and lower the elbow room. Still, for a great steak in a lively setting after working in a quiet place all day, "the zinc" will be a great place to spend Saturday night, or any other night, which will feel like Saturday night at BLT Prime! Without looking up, the overflow of celebratory voices comes toppling over the balcony railings, and one feels surrounded by good times. Looks? NYC sophisticated, a lot of high fashion, entry-level big-time law firm wannabe partners is the look. BLT Prime rocks. Festive. Six-deep at the bar, no one dining yet, and it's only 9:30 on a Saturday night. "By 11:00 the steaks will be served at the bar," so says the maître d'.

As you would expect, this bar has beer as well as a good selection of red wines by the glass. There are six beer selections, a Bud for $6, and climbing up to include a Sierra Nevada, a Brooklyn lager, a Belgium beer, and one nonalcoholic German beer. There are two bubblies by the glass at $17 and $18, five whites from $9 to $14, and eight reds from $8 to $24 for a cabernet sauvignon from the Napa Valley. The appetizers start at $8 for the smoked bacon to $23 for a lobster salad. The sixteen-ounce NY strip steak is $42, and their big seller, the BLT-bone, sirloin double, is $82.

BLT Steak and BLT Prime are a toss-up. Decide by location, try them both, and tell your belly-up-to-the-bar friends which you like best. The corn-fed Angus-certified beef is center at both restaurants, and you choose among the many sauces and sides, creating your own dinner. The desserts (from a

French pastry chef, bien sûr) are above the usual steak-house desserts, so for those with a sweet tooth after their martinis, give the crepe soufflé with passion fruit sauce a try, or the favorite according to the bartender—the peanut butter/chocolate mousse/banana ice cream. Or hey! You're an American, you can even have a martini with your French dessert.

BLT STEAK

106 East 57th Street (Lexington and Park Avenues) *Zagat: 24*
212-752-7470 *www.bltsteak.com*
Closed: Sundays *Chef: Laurent Tourondel*

Midtown chic. Party place, young crowd having fun, noisy in an upbeat way. It's a loud, happy place with men double and triples, with a scattering of women sitting and standing at the bar, very much like The Modern. Be sure you let the bartender know as soon as you get there that you are waiting to belly up to the bar for dinner. The seats are always taken. Your fifteen-minute wait, however, isn't anything compared to waiting weeks for a table reservation. All of that happiness and people waiting for their table raise the conversation level and lower the elbow room. Still, for a great steak in a lively setting after working in a quiet place all day, "the zinc" will be a great place to spend the evening.

Have you heard this before? At BLT Prime? No room for error here . . . it's meant to be. If you change the street address of these two French visions of American upscale steak houses, you won't know the difference. The menu appears to be identical, and the prices, too. This BLT Steak power destination is the first of Laurent Tourondel's (LT) three top-of-the-line bistros (B).

The midtown expense-account folks love the sophisticated luxury setting of BLT Steak's modern black-and-tan decor with flower arrangements to match the Great Hall at the Met. BLT Steak is designed for dining at the bar with fifteen comfortable bar seats, footrests, and like all serious dining-at-the-bar establishments, there are under-the-counter hooks for briefcases and purses.

As you would expect at a steak house, BLT Steak has beer as well as a good selection of red wines by the glass. There are six beer selections, a Bud for $6, and climbing up to include a Sierra Nevada, a Brooklyn lager, a Belgium beer, and one nonalcoholic German beer. There are two bubblies by the glass at $17 and $18, five whites from $9 to $14, and eight reds from $8 to $24 for a cabernet sauvignon from the Napa Valley. Steak and midtown chic have brought you here, even though fish and chicken are on the menu, and so corn-fed, aged, certified Angus steak is what it has to be. Or, if you want to try to recommend the long list of delectable side dishes and steak sauces to your friends, à la carte, go for your drink of the moment with one or two sides and a dessert. The beauty of dining at the bar, remember, is that you can mix things up and eat as little or as lopsided a meal as you want with no waiter looking down his nose at you.

The sides are $9 for the mushroom choices and $8 for the other vegetables, served in cast-iron pans, with selections of eight kinds of potatoes—from shoestring, to cottage fries, to gratin—and the greens include collard greens, garlic cream spinach, and grilled asparagus. The steak sauces are those you would expect and hopefully a few that you haven't had the time to think about, such as red-wine caper brown butter or ginger ketchup or soy-citrus. The night my friend and I were there, we shared a New York strip steak with the three-mustard mélange for $42. He had a cabernet sauvignon from Washington State for $14, and I went for the same. Who could resist a cabernet, the racehorse of the Bordeaux grape, when eating a BLT steak! For those of us who get headaches from the tannin in the reds, just be sure you take your aspirin before you go to bed . . . Don't wait until morning when it's way too late!

The side was too much food, but then, it was the thrill of the steak and perfect red Bordeaux that we were after, and there was not an ounce of disappointment in the delivery. Big portions are an understatement, as this place is the French version of an American steak house, with the emphasis on *American* when it comes to serving sizes. But wait! Let's say you aren't on an expense account and your not-for-profit museum or library or foundation paycheck or book royalty check is in the mail, but you just had to get out into NYC's celebrity-chef heaven for an evening. You can take your time studying that long wine list, and enjoy the duck liver paté and the cheese popovers served to you at the bar as soon as you ask for the dinner menu, and order a side or two with your drink. Give it a try . . . it's a mood changer.

BLUE HILL

75 Washington Place (McDougal Street and 6th Avenue) *Zagat: 26*
212-539-1776 *www.bluehillnyc.com*
Chef: Dan Barber

Don't worry about being overrun with slow-food, greenmarket, organic-types in here . . . you won't even notice after you have your first soup sip or tantalizing taste in this civilized sound level, perfectly lit, small, exquisite, friendly, and NYC sophisticated town house of Blue Hill. It's the parent of the acclaimed David, Laureen, and Dan Barber's Blue Hill Farm in the Berkshires. The smallest rectangular bartender's space held a very tall and friendly David, who was happy to describe the first page of the wine book. And as a student of beer, I have to admit that I had never heard of the Blue Hill beers. The first was an Innis & Gunn Edinburgh ale, aged in oaken barrels. Also an apple beer from Quebec, a ginger beer from Japan, and my choice, as good as it gets, an Acme IPA from Fort Bragg, California. The pages of wines by the glass were priced from $10 to $14. When the man on my right, Jay from Cleveland, asked for a recommendation of a white, he was promptly served a taste of two from which to choose. At the same time, a waiter appeared at my friend Helen's elbow, bringing us an offering of a shot glass of the chef's parsnip soup to taste, which ingratiated everyone at the bar to Blue Hill.

On a Saturday night at 8 p.m. there was a thirtysomething young couple sharing the tasting menu, a young couple sharing and engrossed with every bite, I might add, and three solos at the nine-seat bar. We studied the extraordinary menu while enjoying the ficele (very thin baguette) placed in a tin cylinder before us with farm-fresh butter. We expected to try the chef's art of poaching and braising and made our choices accordingly, starting with a buttercup squash ravioli, which was divided in the kitchen (at no extra cost), consisting of squash set on a creamy broth of poached greens and al dente small chunks of parsnip. The ravioli were unusually thin and dark orange, with extraordinary seasoning and combinations of earthy freshness, crunch, and color. It was hard to believe that anything could be quite that good. We followed our first course with a wild sea bass set on greens, and had decided to move on and try the dessert and coffee at a two-star Michelin restaurant on lower Fifth Avenue. On the other hand, our informant on our right had just ordered the cheese plate, a four-cheese, four nations selection with various breads, and urged us to stay and share. Not wanting to miss out on another tasting experience and able to eat just a bite while still saving space for dessert, we gave in. Other desserts, all at $10, were an apple, chestnut, or pineapple tart, and a chocolate bread pudding.

Our dining-at-the-bar neighbor Jay told us that he had called Blue Hill several times for reservations, but it is always completely booked, and that is when he started dining at the bar for the top food experience in the Big Apple. "And furthermore," says Jay, "it's a lot more fun to dine at the bar," as he is often in town on business on his own. He also recommended the martini, even though he realized that the Blue Hill Farm does not profess to grow the olive. Oh, yes! The last healthy food token was a gift from the chef with our reasonable bill, of a little flower-shaped, dark-chocolate-covered sunflower seed. Very appropriate.

BLUE RIBBON

97 Sullivan Street (Prince and Spring Streets) *Zagat: 25*
212-274-0404 *www.blueribbonrestaurants.com*
Open 4 p.m. to 4 a.m. *Chefs: Bruce and Eric Bromberg*

A small restaurant well known to late-nighters and celebrity chefs who hang out after work as the full menu is served until 4 a.m., with seven to nine bar seats occupied by regulars every day, every hour. Conversation? Forget that! The tables are not crowded together, but it's a very small room, always filled with a lot of happy diners at the bar and in the tiny dining area. The raw bar is in the window, with the dining bar adjacent to it, and everyone is there to relax in a top-food, informal SoHo setting. There were a few more men at the bar than women, and the maître d' agreed that is typical.

It has been said that the best bone marrow is prepared at Blue Ribbon. I bellied up to this bar with a hearty eater so that we could try a few more than usual of these high-end American foods. We didn't want to miss the bone marrow signature dish with oxtail marmalade, and we noticed a banana split on the dessert menu, but wait! Let's start from the beginning. There are several draught beers to choose from, and fifteen wines by the glass from $6.50 to $14.50. I ordered a black and tan while Eric decided to start with a white, the Viognier, for $9. Thinking that the Bromberg brothers sounded like they knew how to cook up an authentic matzo-ball soup, that was his starter for $8.50. Skipping the raw bar for a change, I decided to not stay on the same theme and along with Eric I ordered the spicy fish soup for $13.50. And spicy was the right description! After a few spoonfuls, I offered three-fourths of my forthcoming entrée if he would only swap soups with me. Ah, matzo-ball soup, so soothing and easy on the taste buds. Looking at the menu, which offered burgers to lobster with caviar, a vegetable-K-Bob for $18.50, and a paella royale for $102, we decided to share the toasted pigeon, a first for me, with sweet potato and apple for $26.50. Of course our conversation turned to Hemingway and his living on pigeons in Paris in the poor-writer phase of his life. It was a little gamey, although truthfully I expected it to be even more so—kind of a cross between partridge and squab, I'd say. Eric had a Spanish red with the game bird—a Ribera del Duero, which he has had before with turkey—just right.

Watching the crowd gather, we were glad that we were early, knowing that the numbers increase quickly as each evening hour goes by. By 9:30 it was getting to the raucous sound that we had heard about. No doubt about it, Blue Ribbon rocks! You want more? Check out Blue Ribbon Brooklyn, Blue Ribbon Bakery, and Blue Ribbon Sushi Bar & Grill. It's all on their website.

BLUE WATER GRILL

31 Union Square West (16th Street) *Zagat: 23*
212-675-9500 *www.brguestrestaurants.com*
Chef: Steve Hanson

They come for jazz. They come for jazzy. In an old bank, with winding white marble stairs leading down to the jazz room—candle on every stair, jazz on every night. A very lively place with très chic summer diners lining the side porch, sporting designer fashions and sunglasses in the early evening while checking out the sweet life on Union Square. The upstairs bar at this 1903 Bank of the Metropolis Building with floor-to-ceiling windows and white marble walls is loaded with young, suited professionals having drinks at the twelve-seat bar, with many others standing and grouped around the bar seats. The downstairs bar seats six, with an additional eight in the lounge without reservations that looks out onto a jazz group seven nights a week and draws jazz fans of all ages. They come, too, for Steve Hanson's full menu of seafood, raw bar, and sushi. A very informal group, many in jeans in the downstairs crowd, which is a younger group on weekends, joined by the B&T (bridge and tunnel) crowd out on the town.

I arrived at about 8 p.m. on a Tuesday evening with my independent school colleague, and we took the college rep from Trinity College in Dublin out to show her a Big Apple hot spot. Deciding that the bar would be too difficult for interacting, we opted for the lounge table, which was perfect to see, hear, and share our celebrity chef's specialties without reservations. We were not disappointed! Sarah, our cool guest, loved the jazz, walking down candlelit stairs, and the menu, and she didn't seem to mind that we three were yelling to one another to plan our order and comment on the scene.

We started off sharing the bamboo-steamed shrimp dumplings with a spicy dipping sauce and the tartare sampler of tuna, hamachi, and salmon that whet our appetite for our "being together outside of our offices" evening. With some fabulous seafood choices—we didn't even consider anything else—Sarah's choice was a crab-crusted golden snapper; Rob followed with a simple grilled wild-striped bass and a side order of the lobster mashed potatoes that he wanted us to try, and finally, I liked the idea of a ginger-crusted bigeye tuna, a signature of the Blue Water Grill showing off the Asian fusion with a seafood menu. A bottle of white Napa Valley was ordered to go with the entrées, and we three felt just like we wanted to feel—happy to be having a night out with big-time NYC jazz and the best in food.

BUDDAKAN

75 9th Avenue (16th Street)
212-989-6699

Zagat: 23
www.buddakannyc.com
Chef: Stephen Starr

Now when someone asks you if you want to go to a scene in NYC, know that this Chelsea choice—imported from Philadelphia—is the standard of excellence for full-scale, dramatic, goes-on-forever scene. Eric already knew about Stephen Starr, as he is from Philadelphia, and was very eager to see an NYC version from this celebrity chef. Walk in and let your eyes get accustomed to the dark, and you'll think you've come through the wardrobe to this mystical place. Japanese? Tibetan? Hollywood? They call it Asian cuisine for the downtown chic, fun, and hip. You think I'm exaggerating? Check out the website! A couple of steps up to the high-ceilinged bar space with eight seats plus a lot of lounge places without reservations for the full menu. But go ahead and take a tour of the other rooms, including a huge common table that you can look down on from the dining room. Carvings and objets d'art will steal your attention until you settle down at the exquisite, friendly, easy-to-enjoy bar scene of mostly thirty- to forty-year-olds.

The specialty cocktail? Sin, of course! That's a Hendrick's gin, raspberry sake, sour, soda, and grenadine. Or, for you straight-and-narrow bar diners, a Sacred, which is a cherry brandy, cointreau, pineapple, and soda. Both Sin and Sacred are $10. There are about fifteen wines by the glass from Down Under, France, and the United States. Eric ordered the Rex Hill pinot noir for $13, and I went with the Italian Prosecco for $9 to go with our dim sum, which we were having before we went on to another Chelsea treat for our entrée. The dumplings were just too great-looking to pass up, so we ordered one king crab dumpling and then went for a taste of the signature dim sum, crispy taro-puff lollipops. Yum! Minced pork and ginger, and you'll be so glad this chef moved to NYC where he can get all the attention that he deserves! The man on Eric's right had been often to Buddakan, and he said he comes for the ambience and the Mongolian lamb chops, which he had just ordered (that's with a crystallized-ginger crust). Looking at the menu for my next visit, I'll start with the wok hay frog legs, which I seldom see on a menu, and I am eager to try the chili crab with spicy tamarind crispy noodles. It's hard to leave this Asian theater space, but miles to go before we sleep. . . . It's not easy to keep up with so many celebrity chefs at the Chelsea bars.

CAFÉ D'ALSACE

1695 2nd Avenue (88th Street) — *Zagat: 21*
212-722-5133 — *www.cafedalsace.com*
Closed: Sunday evenings — *Chef: Philippe Roussel*

My faculty colleague Jeff couldn't wait to tell this beer lover about the restaurant with more than 110 beers on their menu! He knew that anything beer and anything French is what I crave. And right he is! This curved zinc bar with more than twelve seats is filled by 7 p.m. every evening with people who want to dine at the bar in the ambience of a neighborhood, high-comfort-level, Alsatian environment, from the outside awning to the tile floors, old seltzer bottles above the bar, and the wall posters, decor, and menu. Even though we looked at the list of more than twenty-five wines by the glass, we could hardly wait to order our appetizer so that we could talk to the beer sommelier, who guides diners through more than one hundred different beers from Germany, France, and Belgium with a scattering of American microbrews.

We ordered the Petatou warm potato and frisée salad at $11 with Alsatian Munster, and La Moelle for $9.75, bone marrow with fleur de sel and toast. There are many choices, but it's hard to imagine a better way to start an evening of Alsatian food than with these two excellent dishes. Jeff had eaten here many times before and often enjoyed the country charcuterie with his beer, and the veal and pork boudin at $8, which several at the bar were eating when we arrived. When we had ordered, we requested the company of Aviram Turgeman, the renowned first beer sommelier of New York City. I'm not a fan of Belgian beers, as they all too often are so strong in their fruit flavors that I've decided only people who don't like beer must like a strawberry Belgium, for example. And I'm also a major fan of microbrews such as Wolaver of Middlebury, Trout River of Burke, and Magic Hat of Burlington—all Vermont beers with everything from porter to light lagers—I don't just take it for granted that European beers are best. Years ago, maybe; but now, not by a long shot! With this in mind, we listened to Aviram, got a couple of tastes as he was more enamored with Belgium than I am, and Jeff, being a classicist, settled on a Belgium Cantillon Gueuze-Lambic, which is from one of the earliest breweries from the early 1700s. This beer is a wild-yeast made with a merging of the old and new yeast years of fermentation. The result is a complex, zesty, and champagne-like beer. Well, it's not from the Alsace region of France, but at least it's French! I went for the Jeanne d'Arc Ambre des Flandres, partly for the label, I admit, but I love the description that Aviram put forth of a beer with a grainy, figgy palate, and a big, dry finish. A very good beer with food. We were both very happy with our first taste, and it was interesting to learn more about our choices.

And now turning to our entrée, even though we could easily have been in the mood for a steak-frites, we agreed on sharing the Baeckeofe—an Alsatian specialty of the house, a casserole of lamb, oxtails, bacon, and potatoes braised in pinot gris with onions and thyme, at $21.50. Oh, boy . . . it was out of this world. We finished off the evening with the Madiant for $8, an Alsatian warm brioche cake with griottes and an espresso, bien sûr! Several diners close to us had come and gone by the time we left, as we talked over every bite and sip, the way NYC bar diners can afford to do with so many choices in so many moods and places to go.

There are many regulars from the neighborhood at Café d'Alsace, which isn't surprising when you think of the few unreserved places there are to go with celebrity chefs compared to the numbers of solo and double discerning diners looking to belly up to the bar every night of the week after a long hard day's work at the big-time business and professional offices of this city. Oh! I must be sure and say that often when I check a website, it is a year old; therefore I was surprised to see that Café d'Alsace's is not only up-to-date, but it is one of the very few restaurants that keep a daily check on their website, even posting the daily specials!

CAFÉ DES ARTISTES

One West 67th Street
(Columbus Avenue and Central Park West) *Zagat: 22*
212-877-3500 *www.cafenyc.com*
Chef: Joseph Paulino

Arriving in the pouring rain after a screening of Woody Allen's latest on the Upper West Side near Lincoln Center, we walked into the warmest enchanting garden with lace curtains, happy groups mostly of fours, every seat taken, confident as we left our cold-soaked coats in the tiny coatroom that there would be a seat for us, sans reservations, because we were headed for the eleven seats at the bar. The first time I had come for brunch at this high-profile, World War I, legendary ninety-year-old restaurant, my friends had been so excited to point out that Mick Jagger was at the bar.

On this night, dining-bar pal Lita and I found the best two seats together at the end of the bar; a single here and there remained at 9 p.m. on a Monday night. The couple one seat away had a delicious-looking grave lox and bread basket placed on a white linen napkin before them. He was a white business-type of early middle age; she was a stunning Lena Horn–looking black wife. A vase with a single red rose sat in front of them; obviously married and still kissing at the bar, they went on to order a three-course dinner, brandy, and coffee. Farther down was a single big man who had obviously been there before, looking like a character out of a Thomas Mann novel who loved to eat. Beside us in a cozy nook for two was a middle-aged country-western-type couple—he, with white dinner jacket and sunglasses, talked throughout their meal; she, with long blond hair, white cowgirl boots, and white jacket with silver sequins, a Dolly Parton look, didn't open her mouth or express any response to his words for the hour they were beside us.

Our "What beer do you have?" question was answered with, "What beer do you want?" "Sam Adams pale ale, and a glass of pinot grigio." Getting very comfortable with extraordinary barbecued peanuts and pretzels before us, menu in hand, we were soon entertained by a very continental, forties-looking man who joined the bar scene on the single barstool to our right. Sporting a brown double-breasted suit, *Atlantic Monthly*

and *New Yorker* in hand, the *Atlantic Monthly* being the preferred read, he ordered a "dessert wine, and a dessert," followed by coffee. As we three were ready to order our food at the same time, he gallantly (befitting his look), motioned and graciously said, "Ladies first." Oh, Woody Allen would have loved it. We are onstage—still in our movie!

We couldn't resist the grave lox, and debated on the pasta of the day—an appetizer size for $14, or the portabella, oyster, and shilli mushrooms in herb sauce; we went for the mushrooms. Amusing, watching bar life and the tables nearest us, gazing at the voluptuous nude murals by Howard Chandler Christy, painted during the depression in exchange for his meals, and visiting with the charming bartender who hadn't seen Woody Allen since *Interiors,* although his fifteen-year-old daughter is a fan. It felt very 1940s and formal, with an older crowd in the dining room. We topped the evening off with the key lime pie and gave it an "8." It could have been more tart, although color, texture, crust, and density were good. Oh well, like others, we came for the tradition and setting, and with a $92 tab for two with tax and 20 percent tip—we got what we came for!

CAFÉ GRAY

10 Columbus Circle, Third Floor | *Zagat: 25; Michelin: ★*
212-823-6338 | *www.cafegray.com*
Closed: Sundays | *Chef: Gray Kunz*

The most elegant, Parisian-feeling café is Zagat's number one brasserie found in the Time Warner complex, just one floor below Thomas Keller's top-rated (Michelin ★★★) American restaurant, Per Se. The regular menu is offered at the nine bar seats and the seven lounge tables with semicircular banquettes around the warm, welcoming brasserie room—the only way to get into Café Gray without reservations a month ahead! The lighting and ambience of the café keep the noise level low, even with several lounge tables around the bar. Besides the restaurant menu, there are also brasserie small plates for those who want to have several tastes of celebrity chef Gray Kunz's exquisite Asian-French cuisine.

It's the dressy place to be, and the evening I was there the lobster salad fit the ambience. Be prepared for the best bread you'll get anywhere and because it's French, you can count on butter extraordinaire. Wine drinkers will have many choices, and the bartenders at Café Gray love giving you samples of their recommendations before you decide. There are about twenty wines by the glass, and half bottles as well. Because I started with the soy-ginger-cured hamachi with cucumber and black radish for $21, I decided to have an Austrian Riesling, but when I saw the wine list with more French Savennières than I knew were produced, I decided that's the thing to try, and so for $14 I enjoyed my first Savennières, from the chenin blanc grape.

There were mostly singles at the bar, although I saw several groups of three with one sitting and two standing and talking over the business of the moment. The lounge tables around the room each appeared to be happily occupied by two or three guests. More appeared to be having their after-work drink at 7 p.m., rather than their evening dinner. Next to me was a Dell rep up from Nashville who was told that her business trip would be worthwhile if she got a reservation at Café Gray the one night she was here. She was enjoying the roast veal, for which she claimed her business trip "completely successful!" Checking out the entrée choices, I was tempted to stay longer in order to try the skate schnitzel; as a skate fan, I could just imagine how wonderful that would be with parsnips, pumpkinseeds, and preserved lemon. Next time.

The veteran regular of Café Gray on my other side claimed he comes for a small plate special and special wine as often as possible to watch the talented chef through the open kitchen. That night he was eager to tell the newcomers to this bar what to try, and he recommended the caramel raspberry mille-feuille at $16, which the Dell rep decided to order; and he was eating the chocolate passion fruit tart with a lemon syrup. I had a taste of each, the raspberry one first, which was just right, before ending the evening with one of the best coffees I've ever had. The Dell rep, the Café Gray regular, and this writer made a cheerful unhooked threesome bellied up to the bar!

CANDLE 79

154 East 79th Street (Lexington and 3rd Avenues) *Zagat: 23*
212-537-7179 *www.candlecafe.com*
Chef: Angel Ramos

I know. I know. Vegetarians can easily get their best choices at Asian restaurants. But wait! That is like ordering a kosher dish from a nonkosher kitchen! At Candle 79 we are talking vegan . . . no dairy! No chicken stock in a pot, washed out, and then used to make wild mushroom soup. We are talking PURE, here. Not only that, but this organic cuisine is gluten-free to boot. Sounds awful to you nonvegetarians? Well, if this carnivorous writer who loves red meat and anything dairy tried it . . . so can you! So give your vegetarian pals a break and suggest Candle 79.

The eight seats at the bar were buzzing with sippers and diners at 7:30 on a Monday night. They were drinking Candle 79 cocktails such as Green Goddess, Carrot Apple Snap, or wine. Diners with reservations streamed into this vegetarian mecca's booths downstairs and its calm, lovely, natural-looking upstairs dining room with few diners over middle age, all engrossed in deep conversation. Friendly greeters are proud of the accomplishments in the kitchen, which you can check out as you walk upstairs, the glass permitting a see-through on the angle, although not straight in from the dining room below, is a great idea.

Raising a vegetarian daughter (not by parental design) and knowing the precision of certainty necessary for vegetarians to relax over their food (no pan used for meat can ever be used again for the vegetarian; no chicken stock is permitted near the soup), I wasn't at all surprised when the maître d' proudly explained to me that before they opened, all of the vents were cleared of the fats, steam, and smoke of the previous carnivorous restaurant. Starting afresh with Mr. Clean, it was clear by observing the diners that there were no doubts about the assurances offered on purity of vegetables without the signs or smells or mists of animal ingredients.

I sat between a "regular" at the bar who lives in the neighborhood, in his fifties, who was just finishing his wine and dessert. On my right were two women in their sixties, and at the other end of the bar there were four young women and one man in their twenties and thirties. The women on my right said I couldn't possibly be there without ordering their artichoke special . . . which I immediately ordered, and yes, it was wonderful with the beer. A good list of interesting beers and the one and only place I've seen one of my favorites, Vermont's Wolaver IPA for $7. As I perused the entrées menu, I thought that my daughter wouldn't believe this fabulous menu and the choices she would have. She would love the cumin-crusted tofu: saffron harissa couscous, eggplant-spinach-tomato ratatouille, preserved lemon for $20. I take it back! No, not the tofu; I am positive that Elizabeth would choose the ancho! Ancho-seared tempeh: roasted sweet-potato purée, sautéed kale, leeks, fennel salad, pomegranate reduction, mole sauce, $20. Being a squash freak, I went with the butternut squash risotto: wild mushrooms, butternut squash, cashew cream, frizzled leeks, $18. Really yummy. The desserts, from $5 to $7, were not up to the entrées the evening I was there, and the ice cream isn't even made with cream, it is made with soy! That's just going too far for a dairy-state bar diner! The truth is, I'm thrilled to have found this prize. Taking a vegetarian to NYC's number one vegetarian bar and restaurant will easily be worth going one meal without the fine products of cows—for the pure surprise and joy of the vegetarian.

CASA MONO

52 Irving Place (17th Street) — *Zagat: 25*
212-253-2773 — *www.casamononyc.com*
Chef: Andy Nusser

There are fourteen bar seats—seven looking onto the chefs at work at the grill, another seven at the bar of all Spanish wines and one Spanish beer—Zaragozana. Do you know it? Of course not! We (that means YOU and I) will have to check it out with Café d'Alsace's beer sommelier. Casa Mono is probably the only place in the United States that serves this Spanish beer in their crowded, small space of forty-two seats including the fourteen at the bar. With the smoke rising from the plancha (iron grill) separated from the restaurant only by the dining bar, and the rock-and-roll sounds blasting from above in a darker than most atmosphere, a memorable ambience is at hand for you, in addition to Casa Mono's having the highest ranking Spanish small-plate specials in town.

Lunchtime is brighter and calmer—with Spanish music rather than rock and roll, according to the bartender, who responded to my question when she finally heard it. Casa Mono is open every day from noon until midnight. You'll know that Casa Mono is serious about dining at the bar, because there are hooks right under the bar for briefcases, bookbags, or purses. There was a young Asian couple on my right, and two young women to my far left who ordered a Spanish wine by the quarter liter (Babbo does that, and this is also a Bastianich-Batali production—as are Lupa and Esca in this book). There are fifteen reds and five whites by the glass—all Spanish. Casa Mono boasts the largest Spanish wine cellar in the United States.

Oh, yes! The Zagat-25-rated food! Well, let's be honest about my food prejudices. When asked what I like, I always respond, "I like everything but tripe and goat cheese!" And the first thing I noticed on this menu was "tripe with chickpeas." Getting beyond those images and observing my neighboring bar diners, I saw the artichoke special on both sides of me, and on my left, a couple from the Upper West Side who often eat at Casa Mono followed the artichoke plate with mussels for one choice and the roasted beet with goat cheese for the other. With the beer order came a white linen triangle for my place mat, ice water, and bread and olive oil, as well as a dish of olives. It was so dark that I had to hold the menu close to the candle to see it, and I longed for the little flashlight provided for that purpose at Blue Hill . . . so don't hold back . . . that's what everyone does. You will want to see every possibility. Having been all fished out from the previous three seafood restaurants during the week, I went for meat and potatoes at Casa Mono . . . but you've never seen, smelled, or tasted meat

and potatoes like this! The steak had been marinated in a spicy sauce and was superb and porter-house-easy to cut; the potatoes were encrusted with onion and lightly fried, similar to hash browns, with a dipping sauce.

Enjoying every bite and the conversation with the couple on my left, I listened to their recommendation and selected the crema catalana for dessert, a signature dessert of a doughnut wrapped around a bay leaf, which was the most fabulous creation I can imagine. I savored the taste while eating it and again when thinking about the taste along with my espresso. Here is a dark, noisy, cramped, smoky, neighborhood top-of-the-line food experience. Go, Casa Mono!

'CESCA

164 West 75th Street (Amsterdam Avenue) *Zagat: 23*
212-787-6300 *www.cescanyc.com*
Chef: Kevin Garcia

Talk about dining at the bar . . . 'Cesca has a whole room of bar! Major seating without reservations. First there is the bar with twelve seats, a sports TV over the bar at each end, and then there are the high, heavy dark oak tables in the center with another twelve seats, very comfortable stuffed-chair-type bar seats, and then there are regular tables by the front window, bringing the count up to thirty-four, and you can add to that four wooden booths along the passageway heading into the main dining room of upholstered chairs, banquettes, and semicircle booths. All of that bar room is without reservations for this southern Italian, earthy, simple menu, offering more fish than meat. It is very Upper West Side (with a French sister, Ouest), meaning it has a neighborly feeling of regulars, plenty of space, and the patrons are not Soho chic! The bar is surely the place to be at 'Cesca. I wouldn't even consider being in those brown-velvet-stuffed chairs and banquettes, with stenciled walls and iron chandeliers overhead—an Italian suburban-looking room—when I could be either alone or with a bar-dining pal in this big, interesting bar room. Besides the two major spaces, there is also a pressed-panini center between the bar room and dining room.

'Cesca is a good place to belly up to the bar after a Lincoln Plaza movie, which is what Helen and I did, selecting one of the unreserved four booths in the bar area so that we could talk about the movie and food rather than watch the game at the bar. The wine list is impressive—suggesting an Italian as most of the wines by the glass were Italian, and there were about twenty reds and whites by the glass. There are five beers, the usual Moretti, Amstel Light, and Stella, along with a DeKonnick, and Brooklyn beers. I went for the DeKonnick as I hadn't tried it before. Helen chose a glass of an aged Chianti; actually it was a Chianti Classico Riservas, and she was delighted with her great find.

We were there on a Sunday night, and therefore had a chance to taste the "Sunday Sauce," the pasta that Nonna used to make in the Italian villages. The waiter suggested the veal shank (as would befit 'Cesca's reputation of Tuscan earthiness), and I have to say, as I saw an order go by, that "hearty" is an understatement. Many of the crowd at the high tables were standing and eating the panini, the Cubano-type pork being a very popular order for the sports-bar crowd. Having tried meatballs at many Italian restaurants, I was eager to taste Garcia's Brodo di Pollo, veal and pork meatballs with fregola and spinach. What a great combination; we chose right—yum! We couldn't resist the Sunday sauce, which on this particular evening was prepared with the house-made chicken sausage and tossed with asparagus and tomato sauce.

I can see why the place is popular . . . if not for my taste in decor, certainly for many of the crowd's taste in food! Kevin Garcia is a great success. Now, of course, we must share a dessert from this celebrity chef: Helen loves chocolate, but she knows that I like other things better, so she graciously passed up the warm chocolate cake and I gave up the rosemary panna cotta, and we compromised on the chocolate-hazelnut parfait, prepared with bittersweet chocolate cream, orange confit, and tarragon. Did I say compromise? You can't go wrong with the dessert selections.

COOKSHOP

156 10th Avenue (20th Street) *Zagat: 23*
212-924-4440 *www.cookshopny.com*
Chef: Marc Meyer

Modern, perfect calm lighting, sophisticated design, corner-drugstore friendly, and serving an outstanding Americana full menu at the bar. Locals plus destination seekers fill the twelve bar seats, which look out at the corner of Twentieth and Tenth Avenues through a floor-to-ceiling glass entryway. A red leather place mat was quickly put in front of us, the glass of water was automatic, and just looking at the menu was a great treat. There are a lot of regulars at this bar who are quick to talk about Cookshop and what to order. Checking out the starters, I was distracted by the curried squash soup with maple crème fraîche and toasted pumpkinseeds for $9. And if I hadn't already eaten, I would have wanted to try the snack of smoked bluefish and toast for $5, which I've had only once at the home of a friend in Sanibel, who had caught the fish and smoked it himself. And certainly I would give a try to the anchovy deviled egg for $4. So many great tastes came to mind and so much pleasure reading this creative menu. The entrées are listed on the menu by sauté, grill, stone oven, and rotisserie. On the rotisserie list were a rabbit dish and a chicken dish, and in the stone oven was a Catskill duck breast, parsley root purée with wild rice, and quince mustarda.

Now who wouldn't want to belly up to the Cookshop bar with a reputation for well-informed and friendly bartenders? And for those of you who haven't frequented Chelsea that much, let me clarify that the Cookshop crowd is much more chic Chelsea than gay Chelsea. As Eric and I had just finished an appetizer, wine, and an entrée, we didn't even consider leaving Chelsea without trying out dessert and coffee at the renowned Cookshop. Much pride in the seasonal dessert menu, which was whisked to our side along with a recommendation for the small rhubarb pie. Lucky we ordered only one! Small for a family pie, but double the size of any single tart or dessert serving at most top restaurants, and quadruple the size of the apricot tart I had just loved at Tocqueville or Falai. Skip the entrée! Go for an appetizer with your cocktail (cosmopolitans are big at Cookshop) and right on to dessert and unusually good espresso. If you've talked about dining at the bar with too many friends who all want to join you for the same evening, sacrifice that social spot and bartender perks and take your pals to the side tables with umbrellas on the street in front of Cookshop . . . a summer night's entertainment of watching the people go by at the hot destination of gallery-loaded West Chelsea.

CRAFT

43 East 19th Street (Broadway and Park Avenue South) *Zagat: 25*
212-780-0880 *www.craftrestaurant.com*
Chef: Tom Colicchio

The flagship of the Craft group (cooking is the craft), this highly modern-style restaurant's look is warmed by leather rectangular paneled walls, copper entities, terra-cotta columns, high floral arrangements, and low lightbulbs hanging from a high ceiling presenting the best of contemporary American cuisine. There are twelve seats at the bar, and by 8:40 on a Saturday night, six of us were dining at one of NYC's top-rated restaurants. A mesh place mat, linen napkin, and ice water were immediately set forth along with the menu, and two friendly bartenders eager to help with the menu. A forties crowd at the bar, although all ages from the oldish (over seventy) down to the youngish (late twenties) appeared very comfortable at Craft.

This restaurant's chef and owner, Tom Colicchio, dares the most adventuresome souls to create their own destination by presenting a do-it-yourself menu, choosing from the best-quality ingredients, pure-depth tastes of in-season specials trucked or flown in daily, combined with the highest cooking skills, to build their own combinations for dinner. The well-informed bartender is willing to help you choose from the fish and shellfish, charcuterie, roasted meats and game, salads, and vegetables in any way you want to put them together.

Starting with a very creative list of six beers, only one of which was familiar, the Victory HopDevil IPA, the extensive wine list had both "New World" and "Old World" to choose from and more than a dozen by the glass. On my right was a young couple tasting the Belon oysters, which are flown in daily from France, and they followed that with roasted wild boar; the man on my left was choosing between the Canadian buffalo and the local pheasant. He wanted to be sure I hadn't tasted either of those selections before he ordered. My only question was, how local did he think the pheasant might be? After that question, he went with the buffalo at $49.

Choosing a beer with an appetizer and dessert was my plan, as I gathered the information for the best choices from the bartender. Having a special interest in top pastries, and having tasted every top pastry in Paris for my book *Paris by Pastry,* I feel confident to say that I know and love my pastries! Keeping the pure and in-season principles in every daily selection on the menu, the pastry chef offered several rhubarb desserts. I debated the pear-and-rhubarb crisp, even as I chose instead the lemon steamed pudding—most of the desserts are $8. Thinking of heavy bread and Christmas puddings when I think of steamed puddings, I asked enough questions of the bartender to learn that this steamed pudding started with a light sponge cake, which was layered with a lemon custard and topped with a crystallized lemon sugar. The pastry was a small circle the size of a hockey puck. This pale yellow treat was accompanied by a slice of lemon topped with an almond-shaped creamy, rich vanilla ice cream. Color was added to the presentation with several small rhubarb jelly cubes the size of dice and two or three slices of that red-orange early spring tart rhubarb fruit. The tastes, sight, smell, and textures came together for a memorable dessert at Craft, followed, of course, by an espresso. Thank you, pastry chef Karen DeMasco; very fine indeed. I knew I was in contemporary American food heaven at Craft.

CRAFTSTEAK

85 10th Avenue (15th and 16th Streets) *Zagat: 24*
212 400-6699 *www.craftsteaknyc.com*
Chef: Tom Colicchio

Want to take an out-of-town friend to the most "only in NYC" testosterone chic and sophisticated bar in town? Want to go back home and describe the stage-set feeling that you get when you enter Craftsteak on the Hudson River? Then hurry to 85 Tenth Avenue in Chelsea between Fifteenth and Sixteenth Streets. Also at 85 Tenth you will be right next door to Batali-Bastianich's Michelin-two-star Del Posto, which has, alas, no dining at the bar. Don't take the lounge tables in order to eat there, though, as they are cramped and pushed back into a very second-class space. Instead, go straight to Craftsteak, look up at those high ceilings, and enjoy this modern, minimalist metal-and-glass bar. Be sure to look into the dining room, which overlooks the Hudson River and High Line, with orchids on each lounge table reaching upward, and a wonderful painting of the same scene that you see out the window.

Settle down at the bar after you've looked over the dining room, the raw bar with twelve seats, and the lounge tables. Check out the cocktails, which include the Ol' West 15th, a passion fruit margarita with cilantro and chipotle hot sauce for $14. There are five whites priced from $11.25 to $14.50, and seven reds from $10 to $20, a French Bordeaux for $16, and a Seven Hills cabernet sauvignon from Washington for $18. Now hear this, there are wonderful draught beers including a Smutty Nose from New Hampshire, a Magic Hat from Vermont, and a Turbo Dog from L.A., for $7; not to mention eight bottled beers. But the surprise is a record six nonalcoholic beers from Europe and the United States for $4 to $7. Must be that all of those finance guys and law partners are going to go back to work after their fabulous steak!

Looking at the menu at the bar reminded me of when I first came to NYC, a friend who was born and raised in NYC once exclaimed, "You always know where your food comes from! You say, 'The trout my dad caught, our turkey from cousin Arnold Tebbets's farm, our butter from Henry Goodrich, our cheese from Cabot creamery, our honey from, etc. etc.'" The

Craftsteak menu reads just like a Vermonter's way of looking at food. The corn-fed twenty-eight-, forty-two-, or fifty-six-day-aged eighteen-ounce steak from Nebraska is $49, $52, or $55. The twelve-ounce NY strip from Pine Ridge Farm in Maine is $39; the filet mignon ten-ounce steak from Knight Ranch, Kansas, is $45. The grass-fed cattle is also identified, such as the twelve-ounce NY strip steak from the Montana Ranch for $48. Not just that, but even the burger and fries cites the cheese from Grafton, Vermont, with balsamic onions for $15. And check out the sides: roasted Tokyo turnips for $10, and Texas onion rings for $10. The desserts are all from the steak-house kitchen's pastry chef, with no surprises here for an all-American list—starting right off with a glazed doughnut, carrot cake, peanut butter cup, NYC's own red velvet cake, or panna cotta, $12 each. But look! No apple pie!

Dining at the bar with twelve very comfortable, sculpted wooden seats is possible, although most of the diners without reservations were eating at the lounge tables, of which there were many and spread out. Some singles as well as doubles and triples were eating their steaks in the lounge area. The hosts couldn't have been friendlier and more welcoming on a blustery cold night in January; you won't even notice the weather when you are entering this splendid example of a big-time NYC steak house!

CREMA

111 West 17th Street (6th and 7th Avenues) — *Zagat: 21*
212-691-4477 — *www.cremarestaurante.com*
Closed: Mondays — *Chef: Julieta Ballesteros*

The friendly bartender didn't look Mexican . . . well no, because he was from Barcelona. And his name didn't sound like a guy's name, Joan, well no, because it's the Catalan spelling of Juan, the Spanish John. Looks and names may be deceiving, but the word out about Crema is not deceiving. It's just what you want: fun-packed, with vibrant twenty- to thirty-somethings at the twelve-seat bar, an open kitchen and a waiting line outside on a Saturday night at 7:30 p.m. longing for a table. Not minding the youth around me, I checked out the beers, all Mexican—Negra Modelo, my Mexican favorite among them—and watched Joan from Barcelona (who has a Mexican girlfriend who brought him to this job) mix up their popular margarita pomegranate, margarita ginger and passion fruit, and his favorite to make and serve, the puma rosado, which begins with a raspberry vodka mixed with cranberry and lime juices in a champagne glass, topped with a sugar-coated lemon slice and set aflame for the serving. I couldn't help but notice and count the tequilas on the bar menu: forty of 'em!

After careful study of the appetizers, entrées, and small sides, I chose the Taquitos de Poblana, three mini flour tacos filled with a pork, chicken, and chipotle mix drizzled with poblana peppers. The presentation was superb: a small rectangular plate on a long rectangular plate, on which were served the three dipping sauces. Eating and looking around and sipping the Mexican beer, one notices the informal crowd, the stylin' mix of blacks, Asians, and whites that reminds one of being in Mexico City, with Mexican music piped in to fuel the excitement. Many singles at the bar on their cells (a very unsual sight at a Zagat 23 restaurant), three were having dinner, although early for a Saturday night. A white triangle of linen was placed in front of me with ice water. Here is an entertaining place to spend an evening along with enjoying superb Nuevo Mexican dishes, prepared by West Coast Julieta Ballesteros, who started her restaurant ventures with the successful Mexican Mama in the West Village. She brings a traditional Mexican cuisine with a formal French presentation, which is like no Mexican you've ever tasted or looked at. For example, when selecting my choice the second time I visited, I went with the three mini tacos again, but this time it was Taquitos Norteños, filled with pan-seared hanger steak, marinated in hojas santa, flavored with chorizo, served with grape tomato and grilled cactus pico de gallo, and drizzled with crema. All of that for $12! The woman on my right said she always has the Tostadas de Avestruz, a fillet of ostrich with black beans, goat cheese, with a guava chile glaze, a $13 starter. I ordered but couldn't possibly finish the Cochinita Pibil Estilo Yucatan, a slow-cooked pork in banana leaves, marinated in a chiote paste and served with pineapple escabeche, sesame seeds, and a black bean plantain gordita, for $25.

You have to see the presentation, smell the dishes, and taste the scrumptious combinations to appreciate this celebrity chef. Crema is also well served by the bartender, who has been at Crema since it opened about a year ago. When you're in the mood for the best Mexican in town, a young lively crowd, and want exquisite formal presentation in the most informal crowd, make your way to Crema!

CRU

24 5th Avenue (9th Street)
212-529-1700
Closed: Sundays

Zagat: 26; Michelin: ★
www.cru-nyc.com
Chef: Shea Gallante

The Wall Street crowd coming together with Fifth Avenue residents appears to form the mainstay of the clientele at Cru, known as well for its fifty thousand wine bottles (one of which goes for $2,000-plus), as for its chef, who specializes in raw-fish crudi, sturgeon with black-truffle sauce, pike quenelles, and poached lobster. You can enjoy the full menu of Shea Gallante, as well as a less expensive à la carte menu at the bar in a no-reservations front room before entering the restaurant. Besides the seven (very high) seats at the bar, there are six tables of two and three persons enjoying the no reservations advantage, and a quiet space where conversation could be heard even in an intimate tone. At 8:30 on a Saturday night, Helen and I were the only ones at the bar. By 9:30, however, the place was completely filled, mostly with wine tasters, enjoying poring over selection possibilities on the list of fifty thousand bottles.

When inquiring of the bartender regarding their usual weeknight bar business, she affirmed our observation that few dine at the bar at Cru. No place mat was brought forth along with a white linen napkin and place setting, a sure sign of few bar diners. Never minding to be the only ones dining at a Michelin-star restaurant at the bar, we agreed to give a try to the grilled quail with guanciale, brussels sprouts, and han-shimeji mushrooms, with a curry emulsion. How about that for a gourmet start? Wanting to try something other than fish that we had heard so much about, we ordered the veal loin cooked with celery root purée, parcini, canaletti beans, and ramps, with a warm black-truffle anchovy aioli. The black-truffle anchovy aioli was worth the visit, and the envy of those wine tasters at the bar as they looked at and smelled our plates!

Nothing on the dessert menu was simple. All had several forms to whatever the dessert. For example, the citrus fruit dessert had a Chinese soup spoon of pink grapefruit on the far left, an organic pear cube, and a purée of light huckleberry next to a small circle of lemon cake. My warm chocolate tart came with a milk shake (the size of a tall shot glass with a straw) of whipped cream with brandy, an oval of ginger sorbet, and a wafer of chocolate brittle. Another option almost chosen was the poached rhubarb with phyllo crisps, saffron-and-white-chocolate mousse, and buttermilk and rhubarb sorbets. See what I mean? Complicated desserts to keep you enjoying combinations of tastes that come together in a celebrity chef's arsenal of surprises.

DANUBE

30 Hudson Street (Duane and Reade)
212-791-3771
Closed: Sundays

Zagat: 26; Michelin: ★
www.davidbouley.com
Chef: David Bouley

Way down in TriBeCa? Wait! It couldn't be easier—only three stops from Times Square on the #2 or #3 train and you are at Chambers subway stop, a two-minute walk from a Viennese experience within the Klimtesque, Hapsburg fantasy world of David Bouley. This celebrity chef has the corner on the market in his three restaurants all in a row. Bouley (two Michelin stars and a Zagat 28; has no dining bar), also on Duane Street, and across the street is Bouley Upstairs (Zagat 25), but no one gets reservations and so it is a free-for-all in the downstairs bakery, sidewalk tables, and sushi bar upstairs. On to Danube, David Bouley's one-star Michelin that has a lovely formal look with informal people, a bar with four seats and several romantically placed tables to enjoy the seductive bar room. The one beer on the menu was an Austrian beer, a Gosser pilsner. The pilsners were developed in the Czech Republic, but at the time that part of the world was part of the Austrian Empire, so no wonder the Austrians make a light, spicy pilsner with a bitter finish as well as the heavier German-style beers. Most of the wines by the glass at $10 to $24 were from Austria, with many whites such as a Grüner Veltliner, Riesling, and Weissburgunder, for which Austria is well known. The Austrian reds were a Pinot Noir, called a Blauburgunder, and a Blaufrankisch, as well as a few French and American wines to reflect the complete wine list. As my pilsner was being poured into a wine glass, as requested, a bread basket man brought several choices to the bar along with a half bar of butter.

Two Israeli men joined me on my left, and as restaurant owners (Miriam Restaurants on Court Street and in Park Slope, Brooklyn), they were eager to talk restaurants and food. Danube is their favorite and they come here regularly. They were having a drink as they waited for a table, but decided to take their first course at the bar so we could talk shop. I ordered the signature starter, a high-altitude cheese ravioli. Before that appeared, everyone at the bar got an amuse-bouche of the chef's asparagus soup served in a shot glass, with a potato cream on top, a shrimp in the middle, and a touch of pumpkinseed oil, which gave it little bubbles on top. Delectable taste, and at that moment would have loved a sip of an Austrian white, although my neighbors said it was great with their scotch. Another time I will order the veal Wiener schnitzel with Austrian crescent potatoes and cucumber salad so that I can see for myself how David Bouley lightens the classic Austrian dishes for which he is acclaimed. I took the word of Rafael Hasid, the Brooklyn restaurant owner who is a regular here, as well as "hearsay." Going for the signature dessert straight from the ravioli was a thrill in taste, smell, and sight at this very enchanting European bar room. Set before me was the Austrian chocolate hazelnut soufflé with raspberry sauce, lychees, and chocolate chip ice cream. Is your mouth watering yet? Are you jealous? You should be! But not for long; get on that #2 or #3 subway and come right on down here and have an end-of-the-nineteenth-century experience for yourself. Don't wait, you won't need a reservation—life is too precious to miss this evening in Vienna.

DA UMBURTO

107 West 17th Street (6th and 7th Avenues) *Zagat: 25*
212-989-0303
Closed: Sundays *Chef: Victorio Assante*

This northern Italian restaurant feels like a restaurant of the 1950s, so old-fashioned in menu and manner. Everyone is greeted with a warm welcome, but it's impossible to get a reservation as there are so many regulars, so belly up to the small black marble bar for the five seats, and you won't be disappointed in the classic Italian dishes with great specials every day. The shock was that they take only American Express . . . no exceptions. Well, cash, of course. I had to jump off that high bar stool and run to the corner to the ATM machine, but it was worth it. Several circular tables with groups of seven or eight at them, every age from the young to the oldish, families with all ages. One table had five women in their forties, and over a few feet was another round table of eight men about the same age.

As it's a dressy, low-key restaurant with about eighty-five seats, conversation works. Even in a group of eight. Feels as if there are a lot of commuters here, people going home to Long Island, New Jersey, and Westchester. The five red and five white mostly Italian wines by the glass ranged from $8 to $17, and the bartender came from a little country near Croatia that he says no one can guess the name of. He loves America and he loves Da Umberto.

Because I was all "beefed-out" from having visited several steak houses this week, I decided against the luscious-sounding scaloppini Umberto, a veal scaloppini with artichokes, porcini, shallots, tomato, and basil for $25, and instead tried their raviolacci, which was exactly what I had hoped for. It was a plate of fresh pillows of pasta stuffed with wild mushrooms in a truffle cream sauce, with a little red cabbage in the center to add color and texture. Light, delicate, flavorful, the perfect dinner followed by a short walk in the neighborhood to end the evening with dessert and coffee at nearby Union Square Café.

DAVIDBURKE & DONATELLA

133 East 61st Street (Lexington and Park Avenues) *Zagat: 25*
212-813-2121 *www.dbdrestaurant.com*
Chef: David Burke

Eight seats, friendly place, all men sitting and standing, most waiting for a table on the Saturday night when I walked into this historic town house in midtown. And what a sight! The dark brown and cream colors with lipstick reds from coral to scarlet startle and smile at you. Lithographs on the walls, a magnificent crystal chandelier, wood cut-out wall dividers, white leather bar seats, and it's showtime on the plates of David Burke. The maître d' told me that on a Saturday night this restaurant serves mostly out-of-towners, the New Jersey and Westchester crowd. Weeknights are the midtown business crowd, who come by for an after-dinner drink at the bar, and often for business dinners. When I commented on the "all men" part at the bar, I was told with a smile that it was a mostly women at the bar the night before. It varies by the evening.

Saturday night with all of those men wasn't what I had in mind, so after a close look around, I left to come back on a weeknight, when the NYC midtown crowd is present, and took one of the four extra bar seats along the plaque-laden wall of awards for star celebrity chef David Burke. Anyone who has read about this restaurant knows that DB likes to fool around with ingredients and make his patrons smile with what he puts before them. I checked out the menu and wine list of two hundred bottles with burgundies and California wines at the center. There are usually six to eight whites, a few more reds, and three sparkling, or bubblies as DB calls them, on the wines by the glass menu, as well as several half bottles. But wait until you see the food list! For example, the pretzel-crusted crab cake at $18 with poppy seed honey and kumquat–jalapeño jam. Most written about is the "Dayboat Sea Scallops Benedict," a spin-off of eggs Benedict with scallops in place of the eggs, and his variation on an English muffin is a potato pancake. Or how about this: a mustard-crusted tuna with bok choy and red curry. The entrées included an onion-crusted roast organic chicken, a seawater-soaked roasted organic chicken for $29, and a mustard crusted tuna with bok choy and red curry for $32.

David Burke is a center stage kind of guy, and many critics don't think that his menu goes with his midtown clientele. This big-time chef isn't always politically correct, in that he says he can buy some prepared stocks and sauces better than he can make them himself. He likes to color things orange. He likes to boil those seafood shells and put them in something unrelated. He likes to have fun! His halibut T-bone is a signature dish with garlicky spinach, lobster dumpling with lobster bordelaise. He likes to make his fish seem like meat. "No ordinary fish fillet for me," he says. "I don't care how fresh it is, there has to be more to it." You can't get a reservation easily at this flagship restaurant because he is so amusing. People seem to like an aggressive show-off that they aren't responsible for. And the food is good! If you don't like the appetizers, go for the scrumptious desserts, ranging from a caramelized apple tart for $10 to the "David Burke Cheesecake Lollipop Tree" for $18, which is served with raspberries and bubblegum whipped cream. You've got to smile. . . .

DB BISTRO MODERNE

City Club Hotel, 55 West 44th Street
(5th and 6th Avenues) *Zagat: 25*
212-391-2400 *www.danielnyc.com*
Chef: Daniel Boulud

Am I the only one who thinks there are a lot of DB's in the world of celebrity chefs? Do you get them confused? Let's see, there's David Bouley, Daniel Boulud, and then there's David Burke! I'm just thankful that Mario isn't named Domonique Batali! Well, we are clear, I know that db Bistro Moderne is Daniel Boulud, of the Daniel and Café Boulud fame. It's billed as a theater district restaurant, but I thought that Fifth Avenue was a long way from Broadway, so if you do go there before the theater, don't wait until 7:45 to run or cab for curtain time!

The restaurant achieves a very hot and modern look indeed, with fire on the red walls (oil paintings of red floral flames), and a young, excited crowd at the bar to match. A fun place to be for the $29 burger at the high-table bar, more a counter than a bar, as there was no bartender, but rather a cocktail waitress. Most were cocktailing on the Thursday evening I was there around 7:30. Loads of people sitting and standing and enjoying Boulud dining and being in midtown where it all happens. Within five minutes I had a seat and checked out the fourteen wines by the glass and beers.

If I had checked out db Moderne before I came, I would have come on a Tuesday night for the Tuesday plat du jour, a bouillabaisse, which if it's this celebrity chef's Americanized French country food, I know it would be as good as it gets outside of Provence. Daniel Boulud has a following for his daily menu, and those who love pork belly garnished with shavings of white truffle show up on Mondays, venison on Wednesdays, wild John Dory on Thursdays, Nantucket bay scallops on Fridays, squab en croûte on Saturdays, and Sundays are Alsatian plates. A typical Boulud creation is turning a dessert into a savory treat, the tomato tatin. Think of a perfect buttery shortbread piled high with roasted fresh tomatoes, goat cheese frisée, basil, and black olives. Having heard much about the DB hamburger and tomato tarte tatin, I decided that the hamburger was too heavy, and learned that the tomato tarte tatin was prepared with goat cheese. Now, I am not a fan of goat cheese, and there is no way around tasting a dish with goat cheese and imagining it without. Lucky for me I saw Mr. Boulud's acclaimed dishes, even as I ordered the Thursday plat du jour of wild John Dory. Have you heard about the ingredients of the $29 hamburger? It is prepared with ground sirloin, braised short ribs, and truffles, with a center of foie gras. But listen to this! You can get a DB Burger Royale with a whole layer of shaved black truffle for $69 or a double truffle for $120. So, you truffle hounds—you know what to do! Rich and fantastic are the words that come to mind.

DEL FRISCO'S

1221 Avenue of the Americas (49th Street) *Zagat: 25*
212-575-5129 *www.delfriscos.com/newyork*
Chef: Clarence Van De Mark

You want to feel corporate America in midtown New York City? You want to show your out-of-town friends how far you've come from Middle or rural America? Then by all means make your way to the McGraw-Hill Building on the Avenue of the Americas to this ceiling-to-floor glassed-in wraparound steak house, located diagonally across the street from Radio City. Circular marble benches surround sapling trees on the elevated plaza, a great place to wait for your belly-up-to-the-bar pal, cell-phone home to check on the family, or just admire the lights of the skyscrapers that headquarter the businesses all up and down the Avenue, and know that the Broadway theaters are all lit up just one block to the west of you. I arrived midweek around 9:30 p.m., and there were very few seats left of the twenty at the bar. It is a big restaurant filled to the brim with the nearby neighborhood people, mostly men, from FOX News, McGraw-Hill, and NBC News very close by. There were several round tables of eight business-suited men enjoying shoptalk and their iceberg lettuce wedges followed by oysters or shrimp cocktail, huge corn-fed, prime aged steaks from the Midwest, and cheesecake. The bartender offered Bud, Stella, Amstel Light, Heineken, and "Sam Adams for the uppity," he said. I went with the oysters and the uppity Sam Adams in a wine glass, but being the only writer at the bar, I didn't hesitate to order exactly what I wanted.

On my right was Greg, a lawyer in town from Texas, who often eats here and had just finished his steak. He told me that when he is out of town he likes to eat at NYC's top restaurants at the bar as he never knows what time his work will be finished, and he deserves a great meal for having to be away from his family. He ordered a coffee and agreed to try one of my oysters as he told me about his favorite steak houses, and that he had been to Del Frisco's in Las Vegas and Florida as well. It's always comfortable, he said, because he can expect the best, great service, and "the waiters never walk away until you've cut into the steak and checked that it is cooked exactly the way you ordered it." He also likes it because it's always bustling with lively people who act like they know what they are talking about.

My oysters were good, but not as fresh as the bartender seemed to think they were. If I returned, I would bring a friend to share a steak and wait to eat my oysters at the Ocean Grill or Aquagrill where they are a lot more particular about their oysters. Greg left, and two women in their late forties or early fifties arrived. When I said I was glad to see more women at the bar, one of them, who often comes here, said she had a hard time bringing a colleague to the bar because women are too afraid that the men will hit on them to enjoy the conversation and great food. I said that she was thinking of sports bar or burger and beer places, because when it comes to eating at NYC's top restaurants without reservations, most people are really into the food of the particular chef and not looking for pickups. The two women worked for the Foundation for Grieving Children, especially children of natural disasters such as floods and hurricanes. Having worked very late that night at a board meeting, they enjoyed every sip of their martinis and every bite of their steaks. And of course, being in a not-for-profit job, they, like a lot of us, want the best food, only less of it, which we can get when we belly up to the bar!

ELEVEN MADISON

11 Madison Avenue (24th Street) *Zagat: 26*
212-889-0905 *www.elevenmadisonpark.com*
Chef: Daniel Humm

"We aim to make this a major dining bar," said the bespectacled, redheaded bartender, who came from San Francisco along with the pastry chef for the privilege of working in a Danny Meyer's restaurant. This classy Eleven Madison restaurant (and the adjoining Tabla) went right to the top along with Meyer's other best Big Apple restaurants, Union Square Café and Gramercy Tavern, and since then, MoMA's Modern. With celebrity chef Humm's experience in creating ambrosia, the art deco look in the landmark Metropolitan Life Building, the thirty-foot-high ceiling with elegant chandeliers and grand windows looking out on Madison Square Park, and the Frank Sinatra and loud jazz sound, the sophisticated thirties-to-forties crowd is hooked.

Forget the possibility of instant dinner reservations. Join the bar crowd for the full menu at this very beautiful hardwood maple bar bordered with zinc, and twelve comfortable bar seats with backs. Start right in with wine by the glass. Daily selections are posted on a maple board above the bar, starting at $8 for a muscadet or Rhone and going up to $28 for a red Médoc. There is a cocktail menu, martinis being the most common. And a much better than average beer selection with draughts of Anchor Steam, Leffe from Belgium, and a pilsner from the Czech Republic at $7. Bottled beers include Sierra Nevada Porter, Duval from Belgium, Fisher from La Belle France, and a nonalcoholic beer from Germany. The drink of choice at the bar is wine by the glass. Silver bowls of smoked almonds enhance the taste.

There are regulars dining at this friendly and welcoming bar, according to my bartender informant. A white linen napkin was placed in front of me; the flatware and napkins from a special drawer behind the bar were held by the bartender. Looking both ways at the bar, I noticed no one at this bar was not dining! Helen was on my right and eager to try Eleven Madison for the first time; I had been there once before but sat at a lounge table without reservations because there was no room at the bar.

This was more like it: sitting up high where we could survey the whole scene, look into the elegant restaurant, and rise above the lounge noise. On my left was a wine director from Babbo, a young Italian guy on his night off, who always likes to check out the competition, especially when it's a Batali vs. Meyer chef! He had ordered the venison and was especially interested in the wine list, as he tasted many, saying that the wine list is as important to the celebrity chef's restaurant as is the food.

Oh, yes, the menu! First of all, there is not one, but three tasting menus at Eleven Madison in addition to the à la carte menu. The first, for $82, is a choice of two savory and one sweet; the second, a choice of three savory selections and one sweet for $96; and then there is the gourmand menu for $145. But for you bar diners, not to worry—you don't have to do a prix-fixe menu, and in fact, you don't have that opportunity. There is a separate bar menu, and that changes often with whatever the chef puts on it from the day's restaurant menu. It's the same chef, same kitchen, so we are still talking (and tasting) Daniel Humm's Zagat-26-rated food preparation at the bar. Choosing first our wine (taking to heart our Babbo neighbor), Helen chose a French red, and I went with a French Sancerre with our shared appetizer, the peekytoe crab with daikon radish, coconut, and madras curry. Hmmm, the radish gave the dish a taste of hot, while the coconut sweetened and added the texture of a great dish. We had decided against the suckling pig, even if it did come from a Vermont farm and had a tempting dried-plum chutney with five spices, and instead decided on the lamb with artichoke and arugula, cooked "à la point" French rare, which lived up to our high expectations. An espresso, more conversation with our Babbo-bar diner, and a promise to go to Babbo next night out, ended our successful evening.

At another time on the weekend at Eleven Madison, it was so crowded at the bar and lounge tables that there was no way we could have had any conversation with each other. So it's your pick!

ESCA

402 West 43rd Street (9th Avenue) — *Zagat: 25*
212-564-7272 — *www.esca-nyc.com*
Chef: David Pasternack

Now this is theater district! And its location doesn't feel NYC; it looks like you are walking around a plaza and entering a one-story West Coast kind of place. But when you step across that threshold and feel the bright yellow Italian lively energy, smell the fresh seafood, and see the hustling waiters around a full house and bar, you know that you are in the Big Apple at one of the great Batali-Bastianich creations (Babbo, Casa Mono, Lupa). This is a small, sixty-seat restaurant with four seats at the bar and another four tables for two in the bar area without reservations. All of the seats were taken when I arrived at 8:15 on a Wednesday night. Waiting ten minutes was easy to do, as it is an intriguing place to be. Checking out the plates going by, seeing who is there, and realizing that I could have a seat in the bar area all made the time fly by. Finally a regular who sat on the end offered me his seat, and he stood and finished his coffee and biscotti as I sat between him and another neighborhood regular, Charlie, oldish—late sixties, early seventies—in the jazz music business; he eats out at a bar every single night. On the far right were two youngish Asian women, thirty at the most. They were soon joined by a handsome young man who stood and had a drink with them as they finished their dinner. He looked like he had just got off a cruise ship, with straw hat and summer cruise wear to match. Charlie was eating the spaghetti with shrimp, which he said was the best pasta on the menu that evening. He told me that he likes Eleven Madison, he loves A Voce even better than Jean Georges, and he prefers Esca above them all.

Victor, the bartender, has been here for seven years and knows the menu. He knows how creative and special this celebrity chef is; he informed me that the chef is an avid fisherman and often serves the special of the day for whatever he catches. By the way, esca means "bait" in Italian, just to show you that David Pasternack knows his fish and what it takes to catch them. Within an hour, two other women came in and sat at one of the tables, one man at the next table reading his paper, two more women, and then another solo man at the end table. All of them were in the middle-age range of fifties and sixties and sounded happy when Victor told them that those tables were first come first serve. When asking who usually eats without reservations, he said that tonight's crowd was typical of the weekly look, and more B&T diners on the weekends—you remember, don't you, bar diners, that B&T means "bridge and tunnel people" from the 'burbs?

There were two beer choices, both Italian, one an amber lager and the other a pilsner; I went with the amber. The fourteen wines by the glass were all Italian and are decantered in quartinis, measuring a glass and a half. I noticed the crudo tasting for $30, as that's a signature of this chef, a selection of six raw seafood tastes in two flights. Then I debated with myself about the baccalà as a starter, as it sounded like the Italian version of the French brandade, a casserole of salted cod and mashed potatoes, which I love, and this was described as poached salt cod, potatoes, and mushrooms for $11. Next time! This time I wanted to try the pasta, so selected the paccheri, which Victor said was an excellent choice. I bet he would have said that with any choice I made! And with reason. This wonderful combination was an artisanal Neapolitan rigatoni with bluefin-tuna meatballs for $21. I had never had tuna meatballs, and it was such a treat! A plate of small Italian cookies was sent out with the bill from the chef. I enjoyed four tastes with a superb espressso. I can see why Charlie, who knows his way around the celebrity chefs, loves to come to Esca.

ETATS-UNIS

242 East 81st Street (2nd and 3rd Avenues) Zagat: 25; Michelin: ★
212-517-8826 www.etatsunisrestaurant.com
Chef: Tom Rapp

Well, not exactly 242 East Eighty-first Street. You have to cross the street to find the bar. This Michelin-one-star restaurant hardly has room for a lamp shade (bare bulbs) and their few tables. The menu specials change daily with the market, and Etats-Unis is known for its food, not the upscale glamour or elegance of its dining room. At the bar of eight seats, the waiter runs across the street and serves you as if he ran to the kitchen in the next room or downstairs to bring back the menu from home. In addition, the bar across the street is known for comfort food. The smell of grilled-cheese sandwiches hit me as I entered on a spring Monday evening at 8:00 p.m. It was packed with people waiting at the door. We are talking small spaces when we are talking about Etats-Unis (United States for you non-Francophiles), not small for NYC, but small for small. The bar across the street has its own menu, in addition to the full menu of the one-star Michelin rating, which includes a lobster club sandwich at $18, stew of the day at $16 with EU-baked bread, baby back ribs at $15, and macaroni and cheese at $11.

There are many regulars at the bar and at the few tables surrounding the bar. If you feel like the comfort of your old hometown diner, all you New Yorkers who are away from home will love the Etats-Unis bar. Very informal dress, a thirty-something crowd with a few couples in their fifties or sixties. No matter the age, it's kickback time on the Upper East Side. I waited about twenty minutes, even though thoroughly entertained by the man in charge (he is as informal as his guests) and standing at the bar having a Riesling from Alsace at $13 while talking to a couple who eat here at least twice a week. There are quarter bottles (rather than by the glass) of six whites from $8 to $15, six reds from $9 to $16, and four dessert wines by the glass at $9 or $10.

Bar tables without reservations are also packed into this place, and many at the door were waiting for a table; we are talking a Monday night, remember. But here is why: On the appetizer list is a twice-risen blue cheese soufflé pudding with chopped chives for $16; on the entrée list is a short rib of beef braised all afternoon in beer and garlic, onions, roasted tomatoes, and fresh herbs, then served with fluffy whipped-to-order horseradish mashed potatoes for $30. But what about this: a baked date pudding with caramelized rum sauce for $12. I chose that one. See what I mean? As I had started early at another dining bar that evening, I decided to go with the dessert and call it a night so that I could bring a friend back to share the seafood paella from the full menu across the street. The following week I returned with dining pal Lita, and we had beer with our Etats-Unis paella with lobster shrimp, scallops, onions, chorizo, baby artichokes, a bit of bacon, and saffron arborio rice for $35. My friend and I were impressed, and that's an understatement! That's the fun of dining at the bar—to share a big plate; and that's the excitement of NYC celebrity chefs—being able to understate the fine, fine flavors, smells, and textures.

FALAI

68 Clinton Street (Rivington Street) *Zagat: 25*
212-253-1960 *www.falainyc.com*
Closed: Mondays *Chef: Iacopo Falai*

Kate, a Columbia MFA student, and I were eager to see what was in store for us on the Lower East Side of Manhattan. Starting with Falai, we bellied up to the all-white-and-crystal bar within the long, sparkling, narrow room, which led out to garden tables for warm-weather dining. The host and waitstaff were especially friendly and knew the menu and wines well, eager for us to be happy with our choice of Falai. With five seats at the bar, very pretty plastic lace mats that matched the decor were placed on the counter, along with ice water and a menu. As we were looking over our options, the chef sent out an amuse-bouche of a pickled-melon-ball gazpacho in a small glass, and we decided that we had chosen well. Thinking about what we could share to have a couple of different tastes, we chose a starter and a pasta with a glass of Italian red, the very fine Bricco Manzoni at $16 for Kate, and an Italian white for me to go with the polenta bianca, a chicken liver, dried dates, and mushroom starter for $12, which was entirely new to us and just what we had hoped for. That was followed by a cocoa-flavored pappardelle; also a venison ragout with black olives for $17. Looking at the menu, I vowed to return soon to try out the Agnello: a pan-roasted rack of lamb with a casserole of baby vegetables and lamb jus for $25.

We noticed that the woman on our left was a regular, as she knew the menu well, and she was eager to tell us what the place is like at different hours of the evening, and different evenings of the week. We were there on a Sunday evening in the early spring, and the garden was already jumping at 7:45. "People back early from the Hamptons," she said. "Those who live in Brooklyn or below Eighth Street." If you are coming from farther away, as I was, and there are so many Lower East Side small, fabulous restaurants to explore, you may consider going to two of them for different courses on your first visit. For example, just a few doors away, and certainly a winner, is wd-50 at 50 Clinton Street, where we strolled for dessert and coffee.

FELIDIA

243 East 58th Street (2nd and 3rd Avenues) *Zagat: 25*
212-758-1479 *www.felidia.lidiasitaly.com*
Chef: Fortunato Nicotra

A fifteen-minute wait for one of the seven bar seats on a rainy Monday evening in April at 7:10 p.m. tells you something about this friendly, top-of-the-line, Italian town-house restaurant. Waiting with wine list in hand to check out the fourteen hundred wine selections, mostly Italian, I was surprised and happy to see the TV and cookbook star and celebrity owner-chef Lidia walk by with her two six- or seven-year-old grandsons, each with a plate of pasta in hand, headed upstairs for dinner with Grandma. The bar stands at the narrow entrance space of the passageway to the coat check and main dining room. Old wood paneling, dim lighting, and a hospitable maître d' combine to "not mind" the crowded bar quarters. All seven bar seats held diners, six of whom were men; one appeared to be a very big regular who saved two seats before several pals arrived, tasted, chatted, and left during the evening. Next a businessman; beside him were two regular NYC bar diners whom I was lucky enough to sit beside as we exchanged bar-dining experiences as well as our food choices.

Wine by the glass provided at least ten reds, whites, and one rosé, priced from $9 to $18; the beer list was impressive with Belgium as well as American microbrews, including a full-bodied bitter IPA, Victory Hop Wallop, for $7. Bartender Joshua was a gracious as well as phenomenal describer of the menu. A white linen triangle was placed on the zinc bar, along with linen napkin and dinnerware, a tin bucket of bread, a glass beaker of bread sticks, and a small plate with three different-colored scoops of various-flavored chickpeas, with a scattering of olive-oil-soaked individual chickpeas. A choice of natural or sparkling water comes with the place setting.

The two fortysomething men on my right had starters of squash ravioli for one, the other an octopus plate. Having watched Lidia prepare her renowned pastas on food channel 21, I wanted to try one of them. After studying the menu of whole grilled fish, wild boar, organs including tripe, much contemplation, and reading the descriptions, I went for the garganelli duck pasta at $22, knowing that the men on my right had chosen two others: the krafi, a ravioli filled with cheese, raisins, veal, and grated citrus rind with rum for $20; and the fuzi, a twisted pasta and tomato sauce with sausage meatballs for $22. Both of them kindly allowed me to taste their pasta dishes. The fuzi was disappointing (he didn't finish it), and the krafi was light, fresh, and delightful. The fourth man down the bar had ordered the other consideration, con cacioe e pere, a pear-and-pecorino-filled ravioli with a white sauce.

The three of us ordered the tiramisu to taste Lidia's version, and we were surprised that it contained no espresso or custard. Her version was maybe one ladyfinger, whipped cream, and a lemon liqueur and apricots. When I asked the bartender if this was what I ordered, he said, "Oh, sorry, I didn't tell you—Lidia likes to experiment, and that is a tiramisu al limoncello, with an Italian lemon liqueur in place of the usual coffee liqueur." Oh. Well, that sounds like what we ate all right. Lucky for us, a wooden container resembling a cigar box came filled with cookies, and a rectangular dish of small light cookies in a row were a wonderful chef's extra taste with the excellent espresso.

FIAMMA

206 Spring Street
(6th Avenue and Sullivan Street)
212-653-0100

Zagat: 25; Michelin: ★
www.brguestsrestaurants.com
Chef: Fabio Trabocchi

There are five bar seats downstairs and eight at the upstairs bar in this swanky Soho Michelin-star town-house restaurant. It has a very upscale burgundy-red and brown interior with leather bar seats downstairs, and an elegant upstairs dining room with large tangerine-colored lampshades, photographs on the walls, and quiet Italian pop music in the background. It's a star-studded-celebs kind of place where you will be whisked up to the second floor in the glass elevator, creating a club or formal look with patrons to match. All ages enjoy the bar upstairs; couples from thirties to sixties find more space between tables there, and a quieter, more romantic scene than the downstairs bar. The upstairs was closed on a Monday night when I first went there in April. I returned later in the week to test out the menu at the entryway bar of the restaurant, which draws the singles, who enjoy watching who's coming and going along with this Michelin-star chef's specials. The downside of an entryway bar, of course, is that when the restaurant is crowded, midweek, for example, it can get very crushed at the bar while people waiting for their tables reach across your shoulder to get a drink and all of those lively kinds of things that some of us don't mind because we like the commotion of life. And oh! You should know that the signature cocktail is a cappuccino martini, straight up, with floating coffee beans.

The bar diners come to taste Fabio Trabocchi's spectacular Italian menu, and to feel like they are having a very special night out, not a spaghetti night out at a neighborhood trotteria, but looking for exquisite pastas such as the prosciutto-laced garganelli—slathered with truffle butter. And so if a seductive Soho elegant mood is yours, make your way with a friend to the upstairs bar, or if you are alone, enjoy the sights and menu at the downstairs bar. I started right off with the signature plate, capesante, a seared diver scallops plate with wild mushrooms, topped with a thrilling taste of brown butter truffle vinaigrette. I felt like an Italian white, and chose the Umberto

Cesari Albana for $10 from their twenty wines by the glass list, which starts and ends high.

I skipped the entrée, although if I had stayed I would have had a hard time choosing between the pasta special or the braised veal chop served with pillows of celery purée, which Kimberly, the woman on my right, was enjoying. She had come down to Soho from the Upper West Side to do a computer demonstration at Apple's big store and decided after the evening's work she deserved a Michelin-star dinner. Kimberly said she was enjoying every minute of it, and often ate at the bar as she usually worked later than her friends and ended up not being able to meet them for dinner. To reward herself for missing out, she always goes to a top restaurant for dinner at the last minute. Knowing that oysters awaited me at Aquagrill, I went straight for the dessert, which I knew from expert hearsay was exceptional at Fiamma. Now don't be put off by oysters following dessert! Remember that the whole point of dining at the bar, besides getting into an NYC celebrity chef's menu without a reservation, is that you can eat as little or as much as you want, and mix up the order of things on the menu in any way you want. What's for dessert? Oh, yes! The signature dessert is a plate of light and airy Italian beignets (like Vermont's raised doughnuts in sugar season) with three dipping (or dunking if we are talking doughnuts) sauces. The three sauces are maple, chocolate, and butterscotch. But of course an espresso must follow all of that sweet.

THE FOUR SEASONS

99 East 52nd Street (Lexington and Park Avenues) *Zagat: 26*
212-754-9494 *www.fourseasonsrestaurant.com*
Dining at the bar for lunch only *Chef: Christian Albin*

Okay, most of you are thinking of dining at the bar when the workday is over. Or at least you are taking an evening break. But in this case, maybe when your business lunch is canceled at the last minute, a client doesn't show up, or you decide to play hooky for a few hours, you will decide to go to the powerhouse Four Seasons front bar. You want to be in the Grill Room for a big-time lunch at the bar without reservations among the other celebs of broadcasting, publishing, politics, fashion, or just plain big boys of NYC. You come, too, to be in the standard of excellence for all restaurants who want to measure their level of pure luxury. Here you will find the restaurant that has kept its first-place status since the 1950s. You'll see rooms that were designed with Picasso on the walls and hand-loomed rugs on the floor; tables with the best of linens and custom-designed flatware; and floral arrangements that befit vintage luxury.

The bar menu for lunch is short and simple, and I have sampled most of it, making my choices according to the season, my mood, or if I am alone or sharing with one of my college admissions colleagues from out of town. There are several admissions deans who call me first thing to see where we can dine at the bar—knowing my favorite kind of research next to college campus cultures is the celebrity chefs' dining bars. Tulane, Penn, and Stanford come to mind. The first time I went to the Four Seasons, my Tulane friend had called beforehand to simply ask, "Where do I get to go on this trip?" He was not at all disappointed when we walked off the street, up the stairs to the coat check, and up the stairs again to the Grill Room. Seated at the bar, we checked the menu as well as what others were having around us to see how their selections looked. Having heard of the wine list, Dave checked out the wines by the glass, about twelve of them plus four champagnes and sparkling choices—he wanted to know all of his options before he chose a full-bodied Sancerre to go with his fish chowder, and I did my usual lunchtime seltzer.

The bar lunch from noon to 2:30 is a $35 prix fixe for two courses. Usually there are three starters, three entrées, and variations of these three desserts: apple pie or tart with ice cream; some sort of chocolate cake; and a creative pudding, such as the orange and chestnut pudding offered the day we were there. There are always oysters for a starter, usually a foie gras paté, and often a lobster bisque or fish chowder from which to choose. The entrée always includes a Japanese Kobe beef hamburger, and usually lamb chops, and Maryland crab cakes or some other fish selection. We'd already chosen our dessert!

We talked shop, supply-side economics on the side of the colleges for high school college admissions. Great for the colleges—hard on families and high school students! And we talked food and NYC. Now when you need to hear the hard news and want to get it in perspective, consider doing so at The Four Seasons. Here is a highly rated restaurant (Zagat 26), which enjoys even a higher-rated decor (27), and a service to match the food (26). Just think, a fifty-year record of opulence. . . . Don't let another fifty years go by before you experience the Four Seasons.

GASCOGNE

158 8th Avenue (17th and 18th Streets) *Zagat: 23*
212-675-6564 *www.gascognenyc.com*
Chef: Bobby Parchment

Feels like home with its six bar seats if you are at home in a French kitchen, or in a writer's world, or in casual, friendly French (not an oxymoron at Gascogne) digs. On a cold, blustery Sunday evening, research assistant Lita and I entered this small, candlelit environment and were greeted with a very warm welcome. We didn't have to ask if we could dine at the bar, as a young man was joyously into his dinner at the same, surrounded by two women, one seated and the other standing, both eating off his plate, all speaking French and English, while they discussed a play the young man was writing. Ahhh . . . this is New York City. This is Chelsea. On the other side of us was a thirtysomething man texting while drinking his after-dinner Armagnac, from the southwest region of Gascogne, from which this restaurant takes its cultural environment: menu, wine list, and ambience. Armagnac is a lesser-known French brandy, but no less a special drink. It must be well aged—that means at least fifteen years—to get the complex flavor that Armagnac is known for: prunes, quince, dried apricots, vanilla, earth, caramel, and roasted walnuts. If you want a tasting of Armagnacs, Gascogne is the place to have it! Besides being known for its southwestern French menu, it is known, too, for its garden, which is lit with Christmas-tree lights in winter, a Christmas tree in season, and where brunch, lunch, and dinner are served in warm weather. The red and white wine choices by the glass ranged from $8 to $13. The beers included the main French export, Fischer beer, an amber that is much more pale ale than lager.

The specials were chalked on a blackboard behind the bar and included a favorite brandade, seen only before by this author in Paris, a mashed potatoes, salted cod, and garlic dish, perfect for an appetizer/dessert kind of Sunday supper. The brandade sang out for a very smooth, lemon-flavored glass of Gascogne's own-label aperitif. We ordered the seared scallops after debating about the rabbit terrine with black truffles. A triangle of well-starched white linen was laid before each of us, with another napkin and dinnerware, a glass of water, and a friendly bartender who works only Sunday and Monday nights. She has been in NYC for eight years, straight from the Eighteenth Arrondissement in Paris. The thirtysomething hostess has been at Gascogne for six years, and her boyfriend is from Paris, and so Paris. Very unlike Paris was the size of the appetizer . . . one person could easily go without an entrée after eating it. As usual at Gascogne, the scallop sauce was prepared with Armagnac. The best crispness, texture, and flavor of the French-country bread, and the creamiest of butter accompanied the appetizer.

In business for twenty years, Gascogne has a distinctive kitchen, which prepares classic cassoulet, as well as the French tradition of organs such as foie gras, veal kidneys flamed with Armagnac, and sweetbreads. Venison, roast pork loin, and lamb were all on the menu. The rack of lamb came with potato puffs, green beans, sautéed carrot, and six good-sized lamb chops. And so, you hungry diners won't be at all disappointed or leave unfulfilled if you head for Gascogne, and those of you who want to share an entrée, Gascogne is the place to do it!

GOTHAM BAR AND GRILL

12 East 12th Street
(5th Avenue and University Place)
212-620-4020

Zagat: 27; Michelin: ★
www.gothambarandgrill.com
Chef: Alfred Portale

You'll know that this highly ranked NYC restaurant (top dozen) welcomes diners at the bar with Chef Alfred Portale's full menu when out of nowhere appears a black wooden tray designed to fit over the bar rail as soon as you ask, "Are you serving dinner at the bar?" And you'll know, too, that they cater to single gourmets and foodies at this eighteen-seat bar, when you look at their four-page wine list of half bottles. Half bottles of red from $23 for a cabernet to $300 for an '86 Pauillac. Not to mention the large number of wines by the glass—reds start at $9.75 a glass and whites start at $9 a glass. Beer lovers will be happy with Sierra Nevada, Anchor Steam, Liberty, and Sam Adams. Foreign beers include three German beers, four Belgian beers, and four English beers, starting at $10. Big bowls of mixed nuts on the bar; the Gotham is known for its downtown New York look and very chic clientele, including those regulars at the bar—traveling businesswomen and -men who spend many New York City evenings at Manhattan's top-rated restaurants.

On the black lace mat and tray are placed a silver salt and pepper set, a fabulous very crisp oval roll with a large triangular slab of butter, and a glass of water—without asking. The entrées from the chef include saddle of rabbit at $39.50, steak at $39.50, the duck breast for $29.50, a shrimp-and-clam risotto for $22, yellowfin tuna tartare for $18, and a salad with quail eggs sprinkled with beet vinaigrette for $18.

Presentation of all the courses is something to write home about. Gotham Bar and Grill gets credit for the tower presentation of food. Some say the chef started his career as an architect, and the signature tower is the seafood salad, which is built up from the base with scallops, octopus, squid, and lobster until it peaks with avocado. My choice for an appetizer-and-dessert evening included the special of scallops with leeks and caviar. There were two huge scallops broiled in butter, two little rounds of potato, leeks cooked down in the sauce and topped with caviar. Yum, it was simply the best.

An English couple in their thirties were drinking cosmopolitans and enjoying the New York City life on my left. Another couple, in their late twenties, were dining at the bar and eagerly observing the action of the diners coming and going. Of the sixteen places at the bar on an early Saturday evening, nine were having dinner, four were waiting for a table, and still others were starting their evening out with a drink and admiring the restaurant. The dessert menu offers profiterole, a pineapple tart, a German chocolate cake, a toasted hazelnut cake, vanilla custard, and a valrhona chocolate bread pudding with chocolate sauce, which turned out to be too much of an undertaking for this one person. Many diners were having a dessert wine, but if you are craving a hearty dessert, this is the place to try it. If you're up on NYC restaurant reading, you'll remember that the Gotham Bar and Grill is *New York* magazine food writer Gael Green's favorite restaurant.

GRAMERCY TAVERN

42 East 20th Street
(Broadway and Park Avenues)
212- 477-0777

Zagat: 28; Michelin: ★
www.gramercytavern.com
Chef: Michael Anthony

Eric, my college admissions colleague from Penn, took the train in from Philadelphia especially to see what great bar I was planning to visit next. As soon as we entered this room with a country-inn feeling, we gave the bartenders the word that we were interested in dining at the eighteen-seat bar, and within seven or eight minutes, we had our places. A very lively,

high-energy, thirties bar, the older crowd was packed into nearby tables in the front room, everyone having more fun and enjoying being out than feeling squeezed into an overcrowded, loud bar room. The dress is mostly downtown informal, although the Gramercy Tavern always has its share of tourists who tend to be more dressy.

The beers included Sierra Nevada on tap, as well as Brooklyn lager and Red Tail Ale; they even had a British beer on tap, $8 a pint. Bottled beer of many kinds including a cider, Czech pilsner, and all the imported beers were $11.50. White and red wines by the glass started at $8 and went up to $17. The full menu can be ordered at the bar of all Danny Meyer's restaurants, but this time we chose the bar menu, which included a grilled lamb sandwich with zucchini, oysters, quail, mahimahi, and bluewater grill. Eric went for the mahimahi, and I was tempted by the parsnip soup, but since soup is hard to share, we decided to try the tuna and beet tartare with sunchokes, radish, and hazelnuts at $14. Great choices! What flavor and texture. It was terrific. Next, we decided to share the pork ragu with white polenta, carrots, and chickpeas for $32, knowing we wanted to go for a major dessert. A brown linen place mat was whipped into place as the bartender told us that about 30 percent of the people at the bar were regulars and he counted on regulars for dinner every night. The dessert menu included caramelized rice pudding with apricot sour cherry compote, a brioche with banana and maple ice cream, and a chocolate tart with blood oranges and ginger ice cream, but truth be told, by dessert time we weren't in the mood for sweet at this lively energized bar, and decided instead to go with a dessert wine and espresso.

The things to remember about this Michelin-one-star bar are that (1) you will want to let the bartender know the minute you walk in that you want to dine at the bar, and (2) getting a bartender's attention ain't easy! Be persistent! Get right in there and belly up to the bar for a memorable landmark NYC dining experience!

THE HARRISON

355 Greenwich Street (Harrison Street) *Zagat: 24*
212-274-9310 *www.theharrison.com*
Chef: Jimmy Bradley

Need to feel especially welcomed this evening? Then make your way to Jimmy Bradley's "other" (Red Cat–Chelsea) restaurant, the Harrison. You will be received with a warm greeting, find eleven bar seats, and be treated like a regular by the servers even on your first visit. A rustic decor, but not too rustic, is in tune with the new American seasonal menu, with background noise that permits conversation without yelling. The walls and ceilings look like whitewashed barn boards. When you sit down at this beautiful blackwood bar in a dining room filled with antiques, mixed dark brown leather banquettes, and modern paintings—a very TriBeCa ambience—you will appreciate the bartenders, who are well trained in the food-preparation descriptions as well as the available beers and wines. You will also say an aha! when you reach under the bar and find a hook for your briefcase or purse. Whenever that happens, you know that dining at the bar is in the chef's plan for his restaurant, and you will be treated accordingly. Looking at the extensive three-hundred-bottle wine list, you will note about sixteen wines by the glass from $9 to $18, in addition to the good selection of twenty half bottles, as well as nine interesting beers from $6 to $10.

When I arrived on a fall evening the bar was busy with happy sounds of conversations and responses to tastes. There were six solo diners, two couples, and, lucky for me, one seat at the bar at 8:15 p.m. After ordering my microbrew at $7, I asked the couple on my left if they had been there before, and the guy on my right what he was eating. I settled on the scallop seviche with red onion, cucumber, mint, and passion fruit for $14 because I didn't see anyone else eating it, and I could check out the fried oysters and homemade cavatelli (duck confit spiced eggplant, fresh chévre) with my neighbors (not that I would have had the duck appetizer with chévre!). I had last had a seviche with my son in Quebec, and this one measured up to my expectations. I could see that the bar diners were enjoying the stuffed loin of rabbit, wild striped bass, and local trout. I wondered what "local trout" meant. In Vermont local trout means from the nearest brook or river, and I had a hard time imagining TriBeCa's local trout! I didn't ask. I would have tried the almond-crusted skate had I been in the mood for an entrée instead of an appetizer and dessert. But I had heard a lot about the chocolate-filled beignets with quince sauce for $8 and also the pear-and-caramel crisp with pistachio ice cream, each for $9, so I went with the crisp because Ted, on my right, was eager to let me taste the chocolate beignet that he was getting, and he had never had the crisp, which changes with the season. Ted, who lives in the neighborhood and eats out at least four nights a week, told me that he always goes to the bar so that he can talk about NYC's restaurants with others, and he said that next to The Harrison, he likes Blue Ribbon and the Public best, both in Soho.

HEARTH

403 East 12th Street (1st Avenue) — *Zagat: 25*
646-602-1300 — *www.restauranthearth.com*
Chef: Marco Canora

You want to oversee the chefs at work in the open kitchen? Then head for the four hot-spot bar seats at the kitchen counter where you can inspect every plate coming out to be served in this delectable Tuscan restaurant, where friendly Marco (who worked with Tom Colicchio at Craft) uses the green market of Union Square in his fresher-than-fresh delightful daily selections of fish and game. You've had enough kitchen in your life? Then you can choose one of the six bar seats or the two tables for two in the front bar without reservations. No matter which seat you choose, you'll see the action of the restaurant or the kitchen and diners in this rustic, brick-walled East Village setting. There's a high comfort level that all ages and varied dress from formal to informal bring to this small space, which was filled on a Tuesday night by 8 p.m.

I joined the kitchen crowd in order to sit with the serious eaters and listen to their dining experiences at the bar. On my left was a middle-aged man who lives in the neighborhood and is a regular at the bar, who brought the attention of kitchen and presentation detail to me. When my eyes or mind wandered from the kitchen to my own plate or the plates of the two thirtyish guys on my right, I learned that these two had tried everything on the menu that evening, while their wives were dining out on the Upper West Side where they live. I made a bet that the women were spending a lot less money than their downtown husbands that evening . . . they didn't take the bet. Right in front of me were eight young chefs—two women and six men—including Marco, who answered questions from the men on my right about adding water to broccoli as they were being pan-fried, or how long to sauté the skate before turning it over, and when to add the salt to the root vegetables.

After much delight perusing the interesting beer list, with selections ranging in price from $7.25 to $15 that came from Belgium, Germany, and the United States, I chose a New York Blue Point IPA. It was lighter than Bass Ale, but the bitter flavor and amber color that I was looking for. The wine list was offered by the glass or by the taste, from $4.75 for a taste of rosé to $22 for a glass of one of the six reds. After much deliberation and advice from Marco and all three bar mates, I ordered the skate, served on a slight coating of parsnip purée that tasted as fresh and flavorful as I could imagine. And my imagination has high standards, as I have had skate at NYC's very top restaurant, Le Bernardin, and at the renowned Le Dôme in Paris. The skate was surrounded with root vegetables and sprinkled ever so slightly with the bright red of pomegranate seeds. Each mouthful was a treat. Besides the smashing success of his restaurant, this celebrity chef has an English teacher wife and an eleven-month-old daughter, both of whom he is very proud of. The family appears to be doing their best in promoting the beautiful things in life, including the opening of another restaurant, the Insieme, at 777 Seventh Avenue, at Fifty-first Street.

JEAN GEORGES

One Central Park West
(60th and 61st Streets) *Zagat: 28; Michelin: ★★★*
212-299-3900 *www.jean-georges.com*
Chef: Jean-Georges Vongerichten

None has a higher profile among gourmet patrons than this très chic Michelin-three-star Jean Georges restaurant, café, and wonderful, lively, thirteen-seat bar, four weeks and three-deep at the bar waiting for a table. Four or five were taking their dinner at the bar the evening Eric and I were there. Sitting on the two end seats provided a wonderful view of the many chefs hard at work behind the windows on the other side of the café. The beer choices included the regulars of Bud, Amstel Light, and Heineken. Mercifully there were other options to include French Fischer, Canadian La Fin du Monde, Brooklyn Pale Ale, Orval Trappist Ale, and Schneider Weisse. White wines begin at $10 by the glass, reds at $11, and champagne from $16 to $34. A young thirtyish after-work crowd was in the café and at the bar around 7:30; it changed to the fiftyish-and-up crowd as the dinner hour approached, and by 9:30, ten were dining at the bar including four solos. The bar café is called the Nougatine Room, with an à la carte menu, appetizers from $12 to $16, and entrées around $26 to $32. We also got to choose from the restaurant menu, which has its kitchen downstairs with a prix fixe of $98, or we could have had the Jean Georges signature dishes menu for $128. Both menus are overseen by the celebrity owner-chef, Jean-Georges Vongerichten, who brings in NYC's top restaurant raves and the very top Michelin award of three stars. Le Bernardin and Jean Georges are the only Michelin three-star restaurants that serve dinner at the bar—not bad odds, considering there are only three three-star restaurants in the Big Apple!

Taking our time to enjoy the beauty of the room with its white marble mosaic floor, high ceilings, lamps on the bar, a wall of windows overlooking Central Park West, and the glassed-in kitchen opposite the windows, we studied the menu.

Slices of light and dark bread were placed before us with a circle of butter, marked with a speck of green leek leaf to designate the salty side from the sweet. Outstanding bread as expected. For an appetizer, we chose the black-truffle-covered foie gras with toast, which came in the shape and size of a golf ball, a little more than the other appetizers at $24. A taste treat from the restaurant chef was one each of a portello mushroom ravioli in sage butter, with a sprig of watercress on top—simply delectable.

Cosmopolitans were the drink of choice at the bar, served in large martini glasses. Watching the two bartenders shake them up and place them on the bar, or hand them over the bar to the standing crowd, we saw a lot of pink drinks going out there. This cosmopolitan bar was standing room only by 9 p.m. The crowd was gossiping, drinking, waiting for a table, and enjoying the smells and sights of NYC's most talked-about top chef.

Before our entrée, a taste of beet tartare with lobster pieces on the side, the chef's signature piece, was ordered and brought to us. The recipe had appeared in a recent *New York Times,* so I knew it had the ingredients of a beef tartare, without the beef. I chose the steamed sea bass with caviar and beets for $26, even though I debated the seared skate. This dish arrived with a red circle of beet concentrate, which had been sweetened with a fruit, and a green circle that turned out to be a concentrate of parsley. Three small beets, short stems still intact, were sprinkled around the beet concentrate. A first taste of the fish proved to meet my highest expectations. Fresh is the word that first jumps out. Add the crunch of the caviar, plus the sweet syrup of the beet concentrate, and all equals a sublime eating experience. We could have had a roasted pear with vanilla beans and licorice ice cream, but we chose instead the bartender's recommendation of a roasted banana petite beurre, with cream surrounding it. Desserts at $12. Ambrosia. Heaven must be like this: always one more layer of unparalleled perfection. A plate of chocolate pieces—a white chocolate-coated truffle and a cocoa-covered coconut— was placed before us. Not one disappointment in any bite all evening long—the Loire white, the red merlot, plus the chef's treats, the black truffle foie gras, beet tartare, plus the fish and chocolate deliver all that one could dream of for an evening spent dining at the bar of Manhattan's master chef.

KANOYAMA

175 2nd Avenue (11th Street) *Zagat: 27*
212-777-5266 *www.kanoyama.com*
Chefs: Nobuyuki Shikanai and Daigo Yamaguchi

Don't want to pay $446 for sushi with a 27 rating at Masa with the Victoria's Secret window in your face as you leave the mall at Time Warner? Don't feel like Masa's second best at Bar Masa? Want to relax among the Villagers in your informal mood (and clothes) in this East Village "best sushi possible"? Watch the chef from the seven-seat bar, or you won't be far away at any of the tables in this tiny minimalist corner restaurant. The whole restaurant is without reservations on Friday and Saturday nights, and judging from my visit on a Tuesday night around eight, you won't need reservations the rest of the week, either. Many regulars from the neighborhood.

Don't be put off by the outside storefront look, which will make you think you're headed for a Chinese takeout. You aren't. At Kanoyama, once inside you'll encounter friendly, young Japanese waitstaff and chefs along with the neighborhood sushi fanatics who value the best in town. I looked in on my way to Hearth one winter evening, and after checking out the menu and the opinions of some of the diners at the bar, I couldn't wait to get back to try for myself—although I wanted to bring a friend in order to get more tastes from the sushi bar, even though there is also a kitchen menu.

Bar-tasting pal Lita and I went on a Thursday evening at 8:30, and we waited only ten minutes for two seats at the bar. It was easy to wait while watching and listening to the sushi chefs and checking out the menu. Notice the beverage menu, because the Diet Coke, Sprite, or ginger ale for $2 tells you a lot about the pricing of this restaurant. There are three white wines at $7 and a half bottle of red at $14; there are six beers, from Kirin at $4 to Hitachino White Ale at $9, which I chose because I'd never had it before. Lita wanted to focus on a sake, and that gave us plenty to think about because we had to read the descriptions of twenty-one different sakes, fourteen of them by the glass, the others by carafes and bottles, all very well spelled out on the menu. We love learning about bar wining and dining, and if you aren't up on the Japanese experiences of sushi and sake, make Kanoyama your next stop in order to get an education! We read all of the sake descriptions and came up with three selections that we tried during the evening, all around $10.

If you are the plan-ahead type and want a foundation of information before you jump in, check out their website. The regular menu is incredible, and in addition there is a section on fish facts, frequently asked questions, and, best of all, the daily fish on the menu. Not only that, but where the particular fish is from! The bluefin toro on July 9 was from Spain, and the red snapper from Japan. If you have checked out prices of bluefin toro at other Japanese restaurants, you will see what the neighborhood buzz is all about, keeping in mind we are talking quality fish here, with a Zagat 27, and you can order omakase sushi or sashimi, "Today's best nine kinds of fish," for $35! We decided on the tasting menu for $55, which included three appetizers, sushi, and dessert. We also wanted a range of tastes, knowing that we could come back as the regulars do and specialize later. Check out that website!

KURUMA ZUSHI

7 East 47th Street, Second Floor
(5th and Madison Avenues) *Zagat: 28; Michelin:* ★
212-317-2802
Closed: Sundays *Chef: Toshihiro Uezu*

You're in the mood for the best sushi in town? The very best (one of only three Japanese restaurants with a Zagat rating of 28 plus a Michelin star)? Even if it's located in a midtown office building on the second floor? You don't care about decor . . . are you sure? Well, with a great expense account or savings for very special occasions, you will find none better than right here—when you walk into an ordinary midtown office building, find an ordinary elevator, and go to an ordinary second floor. Here you will find owner/chef Toshihiro Uezu standing in back of his sleek, simple, modern Japanese design of highly polished red-and-black-lacquer sushi bar with a dozen seats. Some call him professorial—a man who loves his craft.

I went solo in order to ask more questions than I can ask when I'm with a friend, to spend more observation time, and to try to study why this restaurant is on top. The first thing I learned was that most everyone at the bar was Japanese and spoke Japanese to Mr. Uezu, and they had obviously been there before and knew what they were doing and what they were expecting. There was a solo diner in her late forties, and a guy in his early fifties whom I was eager to sit beside so that I could learn about their Kuruma Zushi experiences. I soon learned that the man was waiting for his wife, who soon arrived, and that they were academics from Germany. She is a visiting professor of law for one week at Columbia Law School, and they had a ten-month-old at Grandma's apartment in Manhattan. New York restaurants, a discussion of American higher education, and the whole world wanting to be in America for graduate school ensued, as I assured them that no matter how *U.S. News & World Report* ranks them, Columbia is much harder to get into than NYU. Great relief on the part of the visiting Columbia professor!

It was easy to agree with them that New York has changed in the past twenty years, and yes, the last few Bloomberg years have brought wonderful changes in New York's financial status. Certainly, with the dollar down and the euro up, the numbers of tourists, college applicants, and real estate prices are all high. Even with the disapproval of America's current war policies, New York City is certainly the global city of choice.

We quickly returned all conversation to our food. It was a real treat to sit and watch the chef at work, and then the response of eating jewel after jewel, prepared as it was as an objet d'art. I had heard about Mr. Uezu's warm rice as the base for cool fish flown in daily from Japan, so I asked only for sushi, and wanted one to be the seared toro, which is the buttery-textured bluefin tuna belly that appears to be the prize among the sushi pros. They had come for the omakase (with plenty of money to pay the $300-plus bill).

We discussed the fact that one can't compare Japanese with other ethnic restaurants; the food is just not the same thing. The fun here at Kuruma Zushi is all in the palate, not in the ambience of the place or the decor. Inviting conversation—if only I had met the Germans at Café d'Alsace! As I left my German bar neighbor, he called back to me, "If you're ever in trouble in Germany, be sure to call. I'm a D.A., and my wife's a law professor. We'll get you off!"

LANDMARC

179 West Broadway (Leonard and Worth Streets) *Zagat: 23*
212-343-3883 *www.landmarc-restaurant.com*
Chef: Marc Murphy

French? Italian? Well, let's settle on a French bistro with Italian leanings. Here is one of the few celebrity chefs who welcomes families and children. In fact, while the grown-ups enjoy the gourmet preparation, children can have comfort food. All children's items are $6, and they can even get an ice-cream cone for dessert. Of course you won't be thinking of taking your children to the bar! But that's just to tell your friends about it who never get to go out because it's just too complicated in NYC to eat out often with young children.

This informal, neighborhood, warm decor boasts a bi-level space with exposed wood beam rafters, brick walls, and a working fireplace in winter. The Landmarc has modern booths and art, a signature of TriBeCa. The wonderful circular bar is right by the fireplace, and on a very cold and windy January night, it feels like the only place to be. Not to mention that you can watch the cooks working the grill in back of the bar.

Checking out the beer selections, there are seven beers, $7 each, including a Kronenboug, Sam Adams Light, a wheat beer, and a nonalchoholic beer. Now let's hurry to the renowned international wine list with more than three hundred bottles of varietals. You will soon learn that Marc and Pamela Murphy want Americans to taste new wines as they have always been able to do. Marc, the son of a U.S. diplomat, lived in both France and Italy and was brought up tasting exceptional wines. There are more half bottles than I have seen anywhere in this price range, about nineteen whites and forty reds. The price is right, too, because the Murphys have kept their wine list profits to a minimum in order to give their patrons a wine-tasting education.

Looking at specials for the week to go with that glorious wine, the Spaghetti alla Carbonara is on Thursday nights for an $11 or a $16 portion; the Bucatini all'Amatriciana on Wednesday night; Sunday night is Cacio e Pepe. There are five steaks from a skirt to a filet mignon, all served with french fries and field greens. Just like Craft, you can select a skirt or a filet mignon or a rib eye and then a sauce from six choices including chimichurri, shallot bordelaise, and béarnaise. The steaks range in price from $23 to $34, and they are just one section of the menu; the game and seafood selections are extraordinary as well. I couldn't wait to start off with their signature dish—the roasted marrow bones with onion marmalade and country bread for $12. I then debated on ordering the crispy sweetbreads with a horseradish sauce for $25, but went with my Sunday-night calling of roasted chicken with crushed potatoes and haricots verts with dijonnaise. I had just had too much fish, sushi, and organs all week, and the thought of comfort food on a Sunday night won out. Enjoying my chicken and a half bottle of French Sancerre for $18, I was as comforted as I get, bellied up to a cozy bar on a cold winter's evening and speaking in low tones to the regulars surrounding me.

LE BERNARDIN

155 West 51st Street
(6th and 7th Avenues)
212-554-1515
Closed: Sundays

Zagat: 28; Michelin: ★★★
www.le-bernardin.com
Chef: Eric Ripert

For all of you bar diners who want to try the number one in food for the past five years in all of NYC, the very best of the best, one of only two (Jean Georges) Michelin-three-star restaurants where you can dine with great luxury at the bar . . . here is your chance for seafood through French cuisine, the greatest of all—Maguy Le Coze's Le Bernardin. No crowded space here; situated at the far end of the entering lounge room are five seats with candles on the bar, a few lounge tables in the area, a view of the restaurant, and the only stipulation is that you order the whole meal, the prix fixe of $107 or the tasting menu as you would do in the dining room—if only you could get a reservation!

Celebrity chef Eric Ripert has been at the restaurant since 1994 and divides the fish menu into three categories: Almost Raw, Barely Touched (poached), and Lightly Cooked. Owner Maguy Le Coze opened the restaurant with her brother in 1986 and planned the decor of light teak elegance, museum-quality paintings on the walls, and spaciousness between tables. The evening that I went to Le Bernardin's bar to celebrate the end of my fieldwork and research for *Belly Up to the Bar,* I was more than eager to see what it would be like at the bar, as I had been there a few times before for lunch in the main dining room.

Arriving around 8 p.m., I found a French couple in their fifties who had just arrived from Paris for a week at the opera and theater. They were speaking both French and English and said that when they are in NYC for a short visit, they almost always eat at the bar in order to go where they want to go to get the best. "It is a New York phenomenon," *ils me l'ont dit.* Also at the bar was a just barely forties Toronto lawyer, in town on a regular basis because his Canadian firm has an NYC office. As he was well into his third course, I studied the menu out loud so that I could get his tastes and celebrity chef experiences while in NYC. Checking out the Almost Raw selections, I decided against oysters, tuna, and scallops as I have them so often. I almost went with the flash-pickled scallop slivers, sea beans, and cucumber and pink radishes, before finally deciding on the conch, which was thinly sliced and marinated Peruvian-style in a dried sweet corn. For

the Barely Touched selection, Gordon (the Toronto lawyer) was just finishing a fabulous-looking foie gras terrine with a Japanese seaweed salad that he said he'd had once before at Le Bernardin, and that dish just pulled him back for more. I decided on the seared-rare hamachi, marinated in a spicy Moroccan berbère sauce, with pickled cucumber and mango salad. If truth be known, probably my unconscious persuaded me because of the mango salad! And now for the Lightly Cooked . . . it didn't take long to run through the red snapper, black bass, lobster, cod, halibut, even the skate when I spotted the turbot! I love turbot and can't remember having it in NYC before. There it was, organic turbot from Chile with shiso-maitake salad, and a lemon-miso broth.

The bar is small and wonderful for enjoying the food, conversation, and the celebratory feeling that one gets at Le Bernardin. And now for a French white to go with these wonders . . . I chose a half bottle of Sancerre. Gordon was telling me what he ordered for dessert, the chocolate corn, with three textures, a hazelnut-flavored corn on one of them. I remembered the last time I was here I had the three-caramel dessert with spun sugar, an objet d'art if you've ever seen one come out of spun sugar. I ordered the passion fruit selection, which again was new to me and very seductive in the reading. Let me describe it to you! Passion fruit cream enrobed in white chocolate, ginger caramel, and Mandarin sorbet. Hmmmm. How is that for an enticing finish to the best? And I of course saved a sip or two of that French white to go with the passion fruit dessert.

Back to Gordon: he eats at Le Bernardin's bar every other trip to NYC, he also enjoys Eleven Madison when it's not too noisy at the bar, and he is always happy at nearby Tocqueville, which is the height of civility.

LE CIRQUE

151 East 58th Street
(Lexington and 3rd Avenues) *Zagat: 24*
212-644-0202 *www.lecirque.com*
Chef: Pierre Schaedelin

All that glitters looks and feels like gold at Le Cirque. Find your way to Le Cirque in the Bloomberg courtyard right across from Bloomingdale's. You will find the celebs, the somebodies of NYC, as well as the tourists who follow wherever Sirio Maccioni goes. They know it will be top-drawer sophistication—fashion crowd, finance guys, and politicians—no matter when they arrive. The evening I bellied up to this distinguished bar, which just reopened in 2006 and serves a bar menu as well as the dining room menu, a "Just Married" couple arrived straight from City Hall and were enjoying wedding champagne at the bar. Also at the bar were a fiftyish couple from Boston in town to try several restaurants and theater after he tended to his Wall Street business, two young mothers on my left trying four desserts, and a couple of men talking very serious business.

Friday the thirteenth, the first day of spring break, I was eager for someplace special and easily found it with the best fish soup I have ever tasted anywhere (including Parisian restaurants). Mr. Maccioni himself ushered me into the bar without reservations, and a black lace-design place mat and a white linen napkin were laid at my place. A silver oval platter with an oval-shaped portion of butter engraved with Le Cirque and a silver dish of two excellent French rolls were brought out as I studied both menus. The beer list is impressive, with seven choices for $8, including the regular bar beers plus Moretti and Peroni, as expected, and a Bass Ale and Negra Modelo. There are five white wines by the glass that begin at $13, and eight reds from $13 to $24. Champagne and sparkling wines number six and are offered from $13 to $48.

The bar menu included two mini cheeseburgers presented with fries, sauce, and greens for $18, which were being thoroughly enjoyed by the young women on my left. The man on my right had ordered the Spaghetti alla Chitarra, a seafood pasta, at $22, and he said it was exactly what he had hoped for. At the lounge tables around the bar were several couples having a drink and appetizers, or drink and dinner. One couple nearest me came over to the bar to tell me how happy their Columbia freshman daughter is! They are parents from my school, and as college adviser, I know all of the seniors' parents, although I seldom see them outside our school setting. That was fun for all of us.

There were several triple silver dishes with two kinds of olives and cashews on the bar. I ordered from the restaurant menu rather than the bar menu. The fish soup was served very much like a bouillabaisse, with a silver pitcher of garlicked mayo, croutons, and shredded cheese. The soup was an orange red, piping hot, with several pieces of fish at the bottom of the bowl. A definite seafood and garlic flavor. A definite 10! Then for those desserts: classic Le Cirque stove, and Le Cirque crème brûlée, both signature desserts for $15 and $12. And here comes the petit fours plate, a fontaine, chocolate sponge, ganache, raspberry phyllo, and a pear fantasy, which I chose: a pear mousse over a chocolate cream, fresh pear halves on the plate, with two very thin, crisp pear slices stuck in the top like a cookie. Exquisite, another 10! I'd never seen anything like it. Forget the entrées—go to Le Cirque for fish soup and desserts with your wine or one of the seventeen cordials at the bar!

LEVER HOUSE

390 Park Avenue (Entrance on 53rd Street; Madison and Park Avenues)
Zagat: 22
212-888-2700
www.leverhouse.com
Closed: Sundays
Chef: Dan Silverman

The most important thing to know is that this celebrity chef learned his trade at Chez Panisse, Le Bernardin, and Union Square Café . . . it's hard to beat those credentials! And the next thing you need to know (other than that there are ten bar seats in a little alcove in this dining room, where you can get the full effect of the unusual look of the room) is that the dining room is built in a honeycomb design. You even come through an elongated hexagonal archway; all the honey tones and hues, the light fixtures, carpet design, and wine holders, as well as the shape of the room, carry out Mark Newson's honeycomb motif. It feels modern, and it feels warm, and it feels kind of outer space.

Lever House is midtown and loaded with business lunch patrons, a business drinks-after-work crowd, and business diners. Not that we are not all welcomed! I joined several solo diners at the bar, about six of us, while others were enjoying a drink at the bar. I admit, I was the only woman, so you queen bees out there who want to stand out in the crowd, join me at Lever House for dinner!

You can start with one of seven beers at $7 to $22 from all over the world. I chose one of my favorites not often on the menu, the sixteen-ounce Sam Smith Organic Ale for $12; the twenty-four-ounce Belgian beer is $22. Or you can select one of the four sparkling wines and champagnes from $12 to $25 by the glass, or one of the seven whites and seven reds from $10 to $25. I had decided to go for the beer and an appetizer as I had an 8:30 dinner date, and so had chosen this pricey restaurant to visit for one course, even though I could easily have chosen it for dessert and coffee, given the particular menu. Fish, wild mushroom soup, foie gras, all from $18 to $24 for the appetizers; I chose the fluke tartare because it sounded so Chez Panisse. It was fluke with jalapeño, orange, and scallion. Wonderful with the beer, as well as a choice of breads or rolls with a generous slab of butter.

The man on my left told me that he often has dinner at

Lever House, a walk away from his office, and then goes back to work for an hour or two. Peter (names come quickly while dining at the bar) told me that Lever House has a longer half-bottle list than most, and he prefers a good half bottle rather than a cocktail or two, or a cocktail and a glass of wine. There are ten half whites from $22 to $80 for an Alsatian pinot grigio; and fifteen reds from $35 to $255. Peter had just ordered the rack of lamb, and looking at the menu again I could see the wonderful food combinations in this creative lamb entrée with chickpea purée, artichokes, lamb sausage, mint, and black olives for $44. He said that another one of his favorites at Lever House is the New York State veal chop, which is served in a variety of combinations, but today it came with wilted greens, farro, and baby turnips for $46. The dessert menu listed a fruit financier for the bankers—*financier* is the most popular pastry in the Paris pâtisseries near the *bourse* (stock market). In Paris, it is a sweet almond bread in the shape of a gold brick. The Lever House financier, though, is no little gold brick–shaped almond bread; it is a caramelized grapefruit and gingerbread barbetto, and so good with the Madeira Sercial 1978. So you see, you're in the big time with the big boys at Lever House.

L'IMPERO

45 Tudor City Place (42nd and 43rd Streets) *Zagat: 26*
212-599-5045 *www.limpero.com*
Closed: Sundays *Chef: Michael White*

Location location location. The best part of this bar-dining experience was getting there. Walking across First Avenue and admiring the United Nations buildings and grounds, I had to ask where Tudor City was, and the directions were, "Straight up those stairs. Or you could go around to Second Avenue and not go up those stairs." Stairs are good. Especially when an Italian dinner is the next thing on the agenda. Not only that, but the stairs are pretty and look out on the UN and the East River. And even more reason, it was so like the butte going toward Sacré Coeur and Montmartre in Paris. The stairs zigzag up in stages, changing directions to the top. This whole section of Tudor City, a series of apartment buildings with names such as Heritage and Cloisters, was built in 1928 around a magnificent little park that appears to be on a cliff overlooking the East River. A June evening after the warm rain was a lovely time to be there, and so unlike New York City (as are so many little sections that dining at the bars of NYC celebrity chefs will take you to—from South Street Seaport to the Hudson River to East River and Gramercy Park and so many special sights in between).

Arriving at the restaurant by way of a little fieldstone plaza with a few tables outside, the bar is at the entrance without a view of the restaurant. Scott Conant, who built the reputation for L'Impero's kitchen, left in the summer of 2007, and we will have to wait and see what chef Michael White brings to the menu. There were five bar seats, a baseball game going on without sound, and two thirtysomething women at the bar having a drink, later replaced by a couple at the bar waiting for a table. A young man ordered a beer and asked to take it out on the plaza, where there were two or three tables with an umbrella. When you go, take a friend. I was the only diner at the bar on a Monday night at 8 p.m., even though the bartender assured me that people eat at the bar all the time.

There were huge olives and a bowl of pistachios on the bar to go with the drinks. I selected a Vermont IPA from an interesting list of six beers, and a pasta dish—Strigoli al Nero di Seppia ai Frutti di Mare for $26. It was a seafood ragu on black pasta (flavored with squid ink coloring it black). Maybe one dish doesn't make a rating, but the seafood ragu with a longer than royal Italian name was no Zagat 26! The dessert menu has some interesting choices, all at $9.50 to include a chocolate tart; a banana terrine, which is a chocolate sorbet and sesame nougat; and, for the Italian palates, an olive-oil cake. If I could get the Red Sox game on any other TV, I wouldn't bother going back to dine at the L'Impero bar unless I wanted to show someone Tudor City and the park, which is the best treat of all!

LUPA

170 Thompson Street (Bleecker and Houston Streets) *Zagat: 25*
212-982-5089 *www.luparestaurant.com*
Chef: Mario Batali

Just a couple of blocks from the Angelica, what could lift your spirits faster and be more satisfying than to top the evening off after a foreign movie drama by stepping into the hustle and noisy coziness of this friendly bar with nine seats? You know you're in for user-friendly bar dining when you find a hook under the bar for your briefcase, backpack, or purse. Barely a gray hair in this top-rated Batali restaurant, mostly a thirties crowd, with six diners at the bar, the rest seated or standing, waiting for one of the few tables in the bar room. Walking back to hang your coat, you will see a calm, secluded, conversation-possible small room of diners who appear to be in another stratosphere. Offered a food and wine menu (Italian-only wines and the usual Moretti and Peroni beers) to look at while I waited, I walked back to the coatrack. By the time I checked out the premises, along with the subdued back dining room with a low-measured noise level, and observed the happy clients, the host found me to say there was now a seat at the bar for me.

Ordering the Tappeto Volante beer, a shade darker than the usual Moretti, I studied the menu of wonderful-sounding antipasti in groups of meat and fish choices at $10 each, and vegetable choices at $6. There were pasta specials; the man next to me on my right was eager to tell me of the three veal meatballs he had to begin and a sweet sausage pasta that followed. Pasta seemed too heavy for 10 p.m., so I ordered the baccalà with olives and capers, a salt-cured cod (reminds me of finnan haddie for all of you northern New Englanders, and brandade for you Parisian foodies) served at room temperature, and the buttercup squash with sage and butter. Eager and friendly bartender Bretton was quick to produce a triangular white linen napkin, ice water, and a plate with a rectangle of focaccia with olive oil. He had been a waiter before becoming a bartender, and was well schooled in descriptions of everything on the menu. Bretton knows his wines, and there is a long list of wines by the glass from $5 to $21.

Lucky for me, I sat beside Robert, a lawyer from Austin, Texas, who was eager to tell me that Lupa is by far his favorite dining bar when he is in town. Even though he stays in midtown, he seeks out Lupa for the food, the liveliness, and the high energy of the place; and when his wife comes with him, she likes it best, too. He has tried Batali's other restaurants: Babbo (too stuffy), Del Pasto (no dining bar), and Esca (not enough bar seats), and none measure up to the fun level of Lupa. He has waited from five to thirty minutes for a seat, "but it is always worth it . . . I always get the pasta special, absolutely nothing like it in Texas." And on my left was a local regular, who came in around 10:30, finally someone over fifty-five, in jeans and familiar with the place. He told me, "I never come until 10:30 on a Friday or Saturday night because it's so crowded at 8." "This isn't crowded?" "This isn't anything! You can hear me, right?" He ordered the veal meatballs to start; the bartender was happy to serve tastes of several reds before he selected, and he went on to order the striped bass, served simply grilled, dripping with butter, centered on the plate. Done to perfection, of course—we are talking a Zagat 25. On the dessert menu were homemade sorbets as well as a list of ten cheeses, mostly Italian. As I had just looked at a panna cotta cookbook but never tasted panna cotta, I decided this would be the perfect place to get it right. Simply luscious! Buttermilk, earthy, rich, soft, oozing vanilla, with just a hint of tart from a few stewed cherries on top to set off the sweet cream. An espresso to top it all off so once again, belly up to the bar is the lively way to go in NYC.

And you women over fifty who have yet to belly up to the bars of NYC's celebrity chefs, here's a great place to start because it's so busy . . . you can fade into the crowd and tastes. Women are highly valued at Lupa, which is named for the she-wolf in Roman mythology. Go forth and howl!

MARKJOSEPH STEAKHOUSE

261 Water Street (Peck Slip and Dover Streets) *Zagat: 24*
212-277-0020 *www.markjosephsteakhouse.com*
Closed: Sundays *Chef: Frank Morales*

The only difference between MarkJoseph and the Upper East Side sports bars on Third Avenue is the food. No ordinary burgers, fries, and beer down here with the financial big boys. They gather around a TV at one end of the fourteen-seat bar cheer-

ing for the home baseball team, with a basketball game on the TV at the other end. Walking into this bar located in the South Street Seaport Historic District is a bull, not quite up to the Merrill Lynch icon, but big enough to get the ambience. You will hear a lot of happy sounds from the Wall Street crowd sitting around circular tables of six to eight men with loosened ties and sans suit coats, eating the signature bigger-than-big porterhouse steaks. These steaks serve three or four people and arrive at the table presliced; waiters then expertly serve the slices, getting all of the juices from the platter on each big man's plate. In the bar area are three high tables serving two people at each, not crowding but joining the diners at the bar.

Dining pal Lita and I couldn't wait to try the prime, dry-aged, charred-to-perfection, rare, bone-in porterhouse with the crispiest fries on the side, and another side of sautéed spinach for a little green with that meat and potatoes order. Tito, the Costa Rican bartender, looked and sounded more like a kid from Boston's South Side until he started rooting for the Yankees. His big smile came with the service, and the women waitstaff treated him like their little brother. When our steak arrived, Tito gave us the MarkJoseph service, leaning over the bar and putting our rare slices on each plate, checking to see if it was cooked to our perfection, and spooning the juices over it. No lack of waiter service at this bar!

At the bar on a Thursday night around 9 p.m. were five others dining on seafood appetizers, the thirtysomething woman at the end of the bar with a young man was having the signature starter of colossal lump crabmeat cocktail for $18.95; he ordered the onion soup for $8, and followed with the steak sandwich and fries for $24.95 from the luncheon and bar menu, which is also available in the evening. Another young woman joined the twosome, and she sang the praises of the clams casino for $12, and then ate the fries off the steak sandwich plate. Down the line watching the baseball game, the men were drinking beer and one was halfway through the two double lamb chops from the bar menu at $39.

As you can expect, there are a lot of draught beers at the bar as well as a great selection of bottles and wines by the glass. Desserts were apple pie, chocolate cake, cheesecake, and ice cream and fruit. Desserts didn't seem uppermost in the minds of or on the palates of this bar crowd. Three other diners were all enjoying the porterhouse while cheering and betting for the basketball team at the other end of the bar. By the time we left, two women had arrived at one of the high bar tables, one having lobster ravioli with a tomato cream sauce and the other enjoying her turkey burger. "We don't eat red meat," was their comment. And we decided not to ask them, "Why MarkJoseph?"

We received a final major-league smile from Tito as we left with a promise to return for the very best porterhouse ever presented, smelled, tasted, and eaten anywhere! We didn't have to ask our red-meat selves, "Why MarkJoseph?"

ESTIATORIO MILOS

125 West 55th Street (6th and 7th Avenues) *Zagat: 26*
212-245-7400 *www.milos.ca*
Chef: Costas Spiliadis

Decor is a 10, bartenders are a 10, and the young crowd in their late twenties and early thirties, mostly having drinks at the bar, were certainly there for those two 10s! When I say the place is modern, sleek, and white, I want to highlight white. Sparkling white will steal your attention in this high-ceilinged, big-time corporate, modern-looking restaurant that definitely does not absorb the sound. Your eyes will be drawn to the freshest fish out of the sea, a whole fish display, more like a Greek fish market with scales hanging there to choose and weigh your fish du jour. You will feel as if you are ordering from a fishmonger rather than your waiter as you stand there surveying the catch. The price displayed on the fish is per pound, so watch those dollars.

The open kitchen is visible so you can see where your fish selection will be prepared. Simply grilled or baked in sea salt and served with olive oil and lemon sauce are the preparations of choice. You will realize that the team at Milos knows what they are doing when they put together the best of fish and surrounding ingredients. Most fish are served whole, so needless to say, sharing a big fish at the bar or table is the way to go at Milos. We ate at the bar without napkin or place mat on the cold white marble, while most of the crowd was having drinks. The bartender suggested fish appetizers rather than entrées, which were not encouraged. He said the octopus and calamari were the "most popular," and ranged in price from $15 to $25. We ordered the crab cake, which our bartender said was 95 percent crab with 5 percent Baltimore spices, and charcoal-grilled sardines the size of Vermont brook trout, six or seven inches long.

The beer list will please particular drinkers with Sam Smith and Sierra Nevada on the list of pale ales, plus the usual Heineken and Amstel Light. A basket of thick, toasted bread was served with a dipping dish of olive oil and four or five olives. The coffee was fair, which discouraged us enough not to look at the dessert menu.

If you long for a taste of Greece, then you will enjoy the ambience at Milos with a drink at the bar and an appetizer or two, but hurry on to somewhere else to enjoy your entrée at the bar. Or you could come to Milos after an entrée somewhere else to get a taste of their baklava or berries in season with some of that special Greek honey, and enjoy a dessert wine rather than a coffee. Be ready with your sunnies (New Zealand for sunglasses) and turn down your hearing when you go to Estiatorio Milos.

THE MODERN

At the Museum of Modern Art, Nine West 53rd Street
(5th and 6th Avenues) *Zagat: 25; Michelin:* ★
212-333-1220 *www.themodernnyc.com*
Closed: Sundays *Chef: Gabriel Kreuther*

Oh, boy! When we New Yorkers learned that Danny Meyer was going to be in charge of the renovated MoMA's food services, we just couldn't wait to see what we'd get. The Modern, a very, very classy restaurant in the Museum of Modern Art (MoMA), but also with a separate entrance, overlooks the sculpture garden; and the Modern bar (where you are headed) is right off the film entrance within the museum, and also at the separate restaurant entrance. That is some long bar, and on a Friday night when the entrance to MoMA is free, singles in their twenties to forties flock to the twenty-two-seat bar. And with good reason. Who doesn't want to be in a lively, happy, luxurious, modern destination at the end of the week among kindred souls who at least know where the art is? Whenever I've arrived after a MoMA film to check out this bar, and bartender Brendon, my best informant, and the bar was filled, someone has always found an extra bar stool from somewhere to bring around and put at the end of the bar just for the asking.

You will see fabulous floral arrangements, candles, and that Danny Meyer special—hooks under the bar for briefcases or purses. The small plates, the informal style, and some say comfort food of Alsatian chef Gabriel Kreuther are a hit. And not only for the seats at the bar, but there are also ten lounge tables with a long banquette on one side facing the bar, and a single chair on the other side of the bar defining the bar area, all without reservations. The women outnumber the men, although there seem to be a lot of groups with several women and a man or two among them. Lots of couples in their thirties. Brendon said that I wouldn't believe the number of blind dates that meet at his bar. He told me the woman almost always arrives first and looks around. He asks her, "How's it going?"

and she always says she is looking for someone. Then Brendon gets her name and helps her find her blind date. "Usually they are here just for a drink," says Brendon, "but they see the plates of food going by, it looks good, so they often order. I tell them to let me know if it works out." One of those plates going by could have been mine—I have tried most of the menu at one time or another as this is a place that, like Union Square Café, I just can't stay away from. It's such a natural after a film night to get a small plate.

Start with the drink menu where you will find champagne by the glass from $14 to $27. The nine white wines start at $14 and go up to the Viognier for $23, the nine reds go up to $25 for a glass of 1994 Bordeaux—Château Gruaud Larose. Brendon informed me that outside of the MoDERN MaRTINI at $12, Coming up Roses is his best-selling cocktail, one that was made up at the Modern and named Best Cocktail of the Year in 2005. It combines rose petals, lime, rosewater, Bacardi Razz, and champagne. Beer drinkers will get four draught beers to choose from—all from New York State plus seven interesting international bottles of beer including the Samuel Smith from England ($9) and a Sierra Nevada Pale Ale from California ($6).

As soon as you order, a black rubber place mat will be set in front of you with a white linen napkin, and ice water is served on request. You will love the plate of two rolls and absolutely exquisite country-fresh butter to go with it—go for the butter! Nothing is better—not even cheese—than the Modern's butter. The twin oysters with leeks, cider, and American caviar are wonderful at $12. A colleague who teaches art history helped me taste a few more plates, and he loves the new tastes found in the warm veal and goat cheese terrine for $14. John followed the first plate with the sirloin au poivre with spinach and spaetzle for $19, and I went with the olive-crusted lamb loin with chanterelle ragout, butternut squash, and roasted celeriac for $18. At other times I've tried the poached egg with cockles, Serrano ham, and garlic-almond sauce for $15; the sorrel soup with roasted foie gras and barley for $14; and the tarte flambé for $12. See what I mean? A great variety of tastes that you can afford from a celebrity chef at an outstanding museum of the world. No wonder Brendon loves working at the Modern bar!

MORIMOTO

88 10th Avenue (16th Street)
212-989-8883

Zagat: 24
www.morimotonyc.com
Chef: Masaharu Morimoto

A very young crowd of affluent twenty- and thirtysomethings come directly to this Japanese Chelsea-destination sushi bar, lounge bar, banquettes and tables, and even the communal table. They have to love the modern beige furniture, lighting from the floor, a wall of art: glass bottles that look like tubes, a stage-set with circular walls and lights surrounding you wherever you sit. More than half the clientele were young Asians with as architectural a look as their setting—casual chic, according to the Morimoto greeters. Emphasis on chic, according to JSM. The welcome mat, an orange tent-like fabric, is out from the street, before you enter through glass sliding doors into a warehouse look on Tenth Avenue.

Morimoto was designed by architect Tadao Ando, and the design draws as many diners as the master chef draws with his sushi. When New Yorkers learned that this was to be a Philadelphia Stephen Starr opening in 2006, drama in style was expected (see Buddakan, pp. 52–53)—think Hollywood. Think stage set. Artwork walls of bottles serve as dividers, tables are scattered on many different levels, and you will want to walk in the door, circle the interior past the sushi bar, and then make your way back to the door in order to get the full effect of design and lighting. Do it! It's fun! And maybe the tour will help you settle into the menu, once you are acclimated to this striking environment. Check out the menu, and no matter how high your expectations, the presentation will dazzle you! There are seats at the sushi bar, but most of you "belly up to the bar" types will want to go to the nine seats of the lounge bar, which has a limited menu and sushi. When they say "limited," you will see that you still get the best from this celebrity chef and have plenty of choices.

Lita works at the Metropolitan Museum, so you will understand why she wants to help me out with my research at the restaurants that are known for their aesthetics and design . . . and so we looked over Morimoto from floor to ceiling before going to the lounge bar—which is open until midnight during the week and until 1 a.m. on the weekends. We studied our choices, having decided on a sake because it seemed the right drink for this thrilling Japanese setting. The sakes are listed by groups, and we skipped over the premium and aged and went to the classic group, rather than the sweet or cloudy choices. Checking out the raw bar of Japanese oysters and one-pound Maine lobsters, we decided to order two appetizers to share and follow that with a noodle dish. Kind of the same idea we tried that worked so well at Nobu 57. Saying no to the toro tartare, which was tempting, Lita chose the tuna pizza, which is a bluefin tuna, anchovy aioli, and jalapeño dish; and I chose the lamb capriccio, shiso buds, with a scallion-ginger dressing. For our noodle dish we selected the three chilled noodles, fresh grated ginger, sesame, and shiso.

There were several solos at the bar, and two couples who were mostly eating sushi. You have to see, smell, and taste Morimoto to believe it. You can get the look from their website, which is worth checking out. Japanese graphics at work, and you'll get the idea and the urge to check out this destination experience when you're in the mood for something exciting.

MR. K'S

570 Lexington Avenue (51st Street) | *Zagat: 23*
212-583-1668 | *www.mrks.com*
Chef: Chen-Hua Yang

A rainy summer evening? You want to go out and eat the best of midtown classical Chinese at a luxurious bar? No taxis will be in sight when you leave your building or there will be a long line waiting for a cab at your hotel. So hop on the #6 subway, and if you come up on the northeast corner of Fifty-first Street, you will be two feet from the revolving door of Mr. K's! And you won't care what the weather when you are greeted by the friendly host and see the plush rose-colored bar seats, twelve of them, with an extra four at a high table, all serving the full menu. Oh! You are staying at the Waldorf and want a Waldorf kind of Chinese bar within walking distance? You will find all the luxury and tradition of decor and food at Mr. K's. They are known for their wine list as well as their food, and have extensive French and American lists, with a few other international wines.

The bar is separate from the restaurant, and in high style with a circular bar, filled with a fiftyish and older crowd who carry on conversations without shouting. It's a calm setting in which to enjoy an Asian environment. The long list of appetizers start at $7.95 for two spring rolls, and go up to $15.95 for a seafood imperial, which consists of crabmeat, shrimp, and scallops with soy-scallion sauce in a pastry shell. They also have a stuffed tofu roll filled with mushrooms and vegetables for you vegetarians who seek your fill in a Chinese restaurant.

The list of entrées includes chicken, which starts at $25.95; and unlike many Chinese restaurants, Mr. K's has a few lamb choices along with the pork and beef. But Peking duck is what I was after! And Peking duck it was. Usually it takes two to eat one, but lucky for you and me, there is a half Peking duck for $25.95 on the menu. If I had been sharing dinner at the bar that night, I would have gone for the seafood imperial, half a duck, and a pork dish, but instead, I asked the others on my right and left how those dishes were, and had plenty to eat with my Chinese beer and half a Peking. On my left was a regular, a man in his late forties. Jason told me that he has tried everything at one time or another at Mr. K's. An eager informant, he told me weekends are slow, and on weeknights the bar is filled with diners, mostly from the many hotels in the area. He knows of three other regulars whom he has met many times at dinner, one Chinese woman who works in a midtown office, and two other men who he says also look like they work in midtown.

A formal kind of place where you can always count on a warm greeting, the best of service, and consistently excellent food. Well, what more would you want on a rainy night looking for Chinese?

NOBU

105 Hudson Street (Franklin Street) *Zagat: 27*
212-219-0500 *www.myriadrestaurantgroup.com*
Chef: Nobu Matsuhisa

There may be a higher-rated Japanese restaurant in New York City, there may be better sushi in New York City, there may be New Yorkers who don't like a restaurant tied to a celebrity movie star as well as a celebrity chef . . . but still, Robert De Niro or not, Nobu remains among the top dozen of New Yorkers' favorites. And what's more, it has held its food rating and popularity among the top restaurants since 1994. Nobu is the place for celebrities to be seen, with a decor that enhances the imagination of a Japanese countryside—branches of birch trees outlining the ceiling along with two-by-four beams, as well as a wall of black river stones create a most modern, knock-your-socks-off Japanese calm and peaceful look.

I was there on an early Friday evening in June, and had no difficulty getting my seat at the bar. The friendly waiter and greeting staff are outstanding. Many families were there with young children; like other New York City restaurants, the weekend crowd is different from the weekday or weeknight crowd. My first visit a few years ago was with a group of college advisers out to celebrate our success in getting our seniors into college, and we had made our reservations a month ahead of time, as is usually required. We went for the omakase, and so we got to taste the best of the Peruvian fusion with the Japanese that Nobu made famous, such as the signature dishes of the monkfish paté with caviar, the miso-glazed black cod, and the rock shrimp with spicy mayonnaise. With a crowd, there is always room for dessert for someone. And so I got a taste of Nobu's renowned chocolate soufflé with siso syrup and green-tea ice cream that comes in a bento box.

On the second visit to the sushi bar without reservations, I knew well what to expect. You'll be happy that you are among the dining-at-the-bar crowd, and can just walk right in, first come first served—not to mention being happy with the setting and food. On this particular early Friday evening, I joined a few other solos who were in town for the weekend, and I decided to have a few of those top-of-the-line sashimi as a first course before going on to another bar that evening for my entrée. The choice was right, as I didn't need rice with another course coming, and I ordered according to which fish was freshest at the moment, according to the chef. I had already learned not to put the pickled ginger (gari) or wasabi (Japanese horseradish) into the soy sauce, as was my old habit before being properly instructed by a Japanese sushi chef. If you dip the rice side of sushi or drown the sashimi in the soy, the whole experience will taste like soy. And you are paying for a lot more than mouthfuls of rice and fish in hot wasabi, ginger soy! And so I took a dab of the wasabi on my chopsticks, as told to do, first picked up a taste of bluefin tuna, carefully dipped the end of the sushi (or sashimi—fish without the rice) into the soy, and put it in my mouth with the fish side against my tongue so that I got the full flavor of that bluefin tuna. After eating the sushi is the time when you are to take a piece of the ginger to clean your palate. You'll also be happy to know that this is the time for a gulp of that sake or Japanese beer! Of course, I don't have to say that none of us would dream of washing down that expensive fish with a gulp of beer!

Do you get the picture? You'll love being here; it's so easy to imagine you are in Japan, and what's more, you'll be way ahead of most Americans, pleasing the sushi chef with your eating expertise!

NOBU 57

40 West 57th Street (6th and 7th Avenues) *Zagat: 26*
212-757-3000 *www.myriadrestaurantgroup.com*
Closed: Sundays *Chef: Nobu Matsuhisa*

On your way to Carnegie Hall? Just been to Carnegie Hall? Want to impress your out-of-town business group, relax in the high-ceilinged dramatic bar area of fifteen bar seats, and another thirty seats at the lounge tables without reservations? Well, maybe not relax, but be excited to be among the many Japanese and international deal makers with the best in decor, buzz, and the greatest Japanese cuisine fused with Peruvian accents? Don't want to go way down to TriBeCa? You certainly won't be disappointed in this big-time New York City bar with sake jugs hanging above the bar, wavering rattan walls, and perfect low lighting. The bartenders are friendly and know the kitchen well. Some dishes can be ordered from the upstairs restaurant, although the bar menu from the same kitchen is extensive. There's a page of sushi on one side of the menu and hot and cold dishes on the other.

Our bartender, Oren, said that if we had three or four in our group, to call him ahead and he would save a lounge table. He was quick to ask us what we liked, and he was eager to do the rest. For example, we had belly of yellowtail tuna with caviar for our cold dish, and then he brought a hot dish of squid pasta with asparagus and mushrooms. The neighbor on our left had a huge sashimi salad, the bar-seat guy on my right was just finishing a Nobu 57 specialty of the rock shrimp tempura with a creamy chili sauce, and he had ordered rice on the side. He soon learned that I was looking for one more seat, although my friend had not yet arrived. He said he would sit right there until she got there and hold it for me, and while I was waiting, not to miss the Nobu ale, the best beer option. Needless to say, he was telling the right person!

Everyone at the bar was talking to everyone else regardless of gender or age, all were dressed in midtown office executive clothes, and there were many international businessmen in Japanese and continental suits. No loosen-the-tie steak-house look among the men here! If you haven't yet been to Nobu in TriBeCa and want to try the signature dish that made this celerity chef and his restaurants famous, go to Nobu 57 for the black cod with miso.

OCEANA

55 East 54th Street
(Madison and Park Avenues) *Zagat: 26; Michelin: ★*
212-759-5941 *www.oceanarestaurant.com*
Closed: Sundays *Chef: Ben Pollinger*

It's ship ahoy on a luxury ocean liner. The key word here is luxury: in looks, service, presentation, and freshest-of-the-fresh fish and seafood. The decor, design, menu, and even portholes with scenes of the ocean and passing ships come together with a Michelin one-star to bring you oceans of the best of shellfish and fish. The small bar room upstairs with four seats and two tables is popular during the week for an after-work drink, with many standing as well as sitting at the bar. A special menu of oysters, cheeses, and sashimi is offered for before dinner or starters. The full menu is available at the bar, but seldom ordered. The midtown business New Yorkers and out-of-towners usually have reservations for a table in the dining room with a six-course tasting menu or an à la carte lunch menu.

My first visit was a little after eight on a Saturday night in May after a MoMA film. It was so quiet in the restaurant, and with no one at the bar, there was no way I was going to stick around to check out anything! I returned at the same time on a Tuesday evening in June, and found mostly champagne and raw-bar diners for their after-deal-making snack before going on to dinner. There was one diner doing the whole menu, but this is a drinking and oysters bar for the most part. But hey! That's okay. I like oysters, don't you? And at this raw bar, you can get oysters on the half shell with a dollop of caviar.

Your taste buds will tell you that this celebrity chef knows what he is doing. He is known for showy foods and mixtures with seafood that are unheard of. Not only French, but Asian and Indian influences creep into his preparations as well. He is a creative kind of guy who likes doing something new. Pollinger has many fans who work in midtown and are regulars just to see what he will come up with next. I have a feeling that besides Paris, he may have spent some time in Normandy, as calvados, apples, and cider are often integrated into his preparations. The regular beside me at the bar was describing his scallops, which were caramelized and mixed with pumpkin and walnuts, and sprayed with apple cider. See what I mean? Where else would you find such interesting sea fare unless you're on a pal's private yacht with a celebrity chef in the galley!

If you go to the bar and want to read rather than visit with the bartender or other bar diners, just ask for the wine list. There are more than twenty-five thousand international bottles in Oceana's cellar, and one thousand–plus different labels with many by the glass and half bottle. If you aren't invited on that private yacht, why not give this royal experience a once-over and find out what it's like.

OCEAN GRILL

384 Columbus Avenue (78th and 79th Streets) *Zagat: 23*
212-579-2300 *www.brguestrestaurants.com*
Chef: Steve Hanson

You'll know Ocean Grill rocks the moment you walk in from the street-level entrance, directly across from the Museum of Natural History. Check out the main dining deck; observe the shells covering the ceiling lights to perfection, and the portholes to check the kitchen level. Take a port to the bar room, and ahoy . . . you will find twelve seats around a beautiful mahogany bar, three or four on the sidewall, and tables seating about thirty-five more people without reservations around the bar. Packed on a Friday night at seven, it was no less lively in the main dining room than in the bar, filled with loud, happy sounds coming from the mouths of thirty- and fortysomethings of the Upper West Side. Black-and-white photos decorate the walls, adding seashore sights, and the friendly bartender says that regulars take at least a third of the bar seats most evenings.

Although 7:00 was early for this crowd to be thinking of dinner on a Friday night, we were off to a reading at Columbia's graduate creative writing program, so all were prepared to eat early. First on the dining list is an array of oysters arriving daily (and taste attests to the truth of this statement) from the East and West Coasts. The bartender helps in the selection when asked for a description of the brine level and size of each oyster. I seldom have had fresher, colder oysters and never better away from the North Sea. An incredible menu of simply grilled, with choice of sides (bok choy and shiitake mushrooms, and a variety of salsas) and sauces, ginger-soy vinaigrette, olive tarape, sun-dried tomato, or specials to include Maine lobsters, and all kinds of maki rolls. Best for bar diners, one can order a single oyster or maki roll! A nice change to be able to have three oysters instead of six for those of us who like to try a variety of the chef's preparations.

A Vermont pal had driven seven hours south to see what she has been missing in the Big Apple, and since it was the early days of spring, with no trips to Maine since last summer, seafood was uppermost on her mind. We started with oysters and maki rolls, and went to a platter of grilled shrimp and scallops, with a side of the special corn salsa and the olive tarape. We decided that our order wouldn't be enough, so we added a half pound of Jaha crab served on cracked ice. Yummmm.

Oh, yes, the beer! Sierra Nevada was the beer of choice; nothing special on the beer list. Wanting just a taste of sweet, as we had ordered almost too much, we had often had maple brûlée in Vermont, and sometimes chocolate, but never espresso chocolate brûlée. It was scrumptious! A bitterness in the caramelized mixture of sugar and espresso on top, and a very deep intense flavor of chocolate brûlée underneath, reminding me of chocolate in France with a higher concentration of cocoa and less sugar than the American version.

Even though the place is crowded and the noise level high, it's a very festive crowd and noise level, which after all should be expected when a place rocks!

THE ORCHARD

162 Orchard Street (Rivington and Stanton Streets) *Zagat: 24*
212-353-3570 *www.theorchardny.com*
Closed: Sundays *Chef: John LaFemina*

Destination: Lower East Side! Top rated of the group of best in the neighborhood is the Orchard—modern, contemporary, and funky enough to attract Brooklynites along with the dressed-down and dressed-up crowd. Kind of like the young, diverse, Crema crowd. There are so few celebrity chefs who can bring in all kinds of people, you can count them on one hand.

I first checked out the Orchard on a Sunday evening; don't make that mistake! But I was pleased to see menus available outside, and knew enough to return on any day but Sunday. There are eight seats at this bar, and wait until you see them . . . a great-looking wood bar where you can check out the whole restaurant and get the full ambience and see what's doing. A list of seven beers, including international, from $7 to $12, and about eight wines by the glass. The Orchard is a place where it's hard to get a reservation and several couples were dining at the bar, leaving a few single seats. The evening I went there around 7:30 I found a seat right away, but by 8:30 it would have been hard to do. This place jumps with joy of location, small size, sophisticated interior with their solid light-wood furniture, modern lamps, tall floral arrangement on the end of the bar, and very, very friendly waitstaff.

Deciding on a glass of Prosecco de Veneto for $11 because it's so the thing to drink these days in NYC, I wanted to see what the buzz was all about. I learned that this particular wine comes from the Prosecco grape, with a little pinot grigio thrown in from the vineyards just north of Venice. It used to be slightly sweet and slightly bubbly, but marketing to today's crowd, it is now dry and much more spumante. Why is it always cheaper than champagne? Because it gets its bubbles from a second fermentation in pressurized tanks rather than in individual bottles, and it is a little more fruity and less crisp than champagne. Still, for the price, there is high interest in Prosecco, and now I understand why!

The menu—the menu—oh, yes, on to the menu. I checked out the flatbreads from $11 to $13 that I had heard about, but decided I'd rather try an entrée and go for the dessert rather than more bread. The woman on my right had a filet-mignon wrap for $15, to give you an idea of the menu, and I was tempted by the smoked trout tartlet for $14, which I had seen only on a menu in Vermont. However, I stuck to my plan and ordered—listen to this—olive-oil-poached halibut, crispy artichoke hearts, and lemon confit for $27. Does that sound creative, crunchy, healthy, fab? Every bite was a treat. Does it sound like a perfect dish to go with a glass of Proscecco? I thought so.

After much talk and eating as slowly as possible, I checked out the $10 dessert menu and was intrigued by the churros—fried doughnut sticks with chocolate and dipping sauces. It reminded me of Casa Mono and their doughnut around a bay leaf with dipping sauces. Great combinations this evening. And a Zagat 24 at its height for every single thing tasted. I can't wait to bring a belly-up-to-the-bar pal with me next time and try a few more tastes from this inventive contemporary menu.

OUEST

2315 Broadway (83rd and 84th Streets)
212-580-8700

Zagat: 25
www.ouestny.com
Chef: Tom Valenti

The Upper West Side! Come on up . . . come on over. The neighborhood Americana, in with a 25 rating, provides people-watching in the nearby red leather booths or even a few TV sports-bar opportunities with eight red leather bar seats. Tom Valenti is known for his comfort slow-cooked roasts of pork, chicken, and duck with mashed potatoes and root veggies. Grilled pork chops and grilled lamb chops are among the popular simply grilled selections, and you don't have to worry about taking a vegetarian along, as the chef often has one vegetarian plate for the odd one out, or will happily put all of those root veggies together.

I had been to Ouest once before in a group of six, packed into the balcony with low ceilings. A dark setting with nothing to look at or see and just noise to hear is no fun. And therefore I was looking forward to my favorite spot in a restaurant when on a November evening I met my Upper West Side friend Marcie at the wood-paneled bar with soft lighting and high ceiling fans. Marcie is a faculty colleague who proudly hails Ouest as the best of the West. We had a lot to talk about, as colleagues do, and found one bar seat (can't neglect the bar research, after all!), but within ten minutes we had our two seats together. With the sports TV playing overhead, and a high noise level at the bar, we were prepared to talk as loudly as necessary to gossip and to get caught up with each other.

There was a nice selection of beers, starting at $7 to $14 for a few of the international beers. I went for one of my favorites, Anchor Steam, since there were no new IPAs to try. Marcie had a choice of ten red wines by the glass from $9 to $16, and she selected a Spanish red. There was skate and also halibut on the menu, with sides of white-bean purée and polenta. The French side of the menu is represented by the rabbit, tripe, and steak-frites. Meat loaf is usually on the menu to comfort the neighborhood crowd, and Tom Valenti is famous for his short ribs and his pork and lamb shanks. The regular we spoke to at the bar told us that he looks forward to the lamb shanks special, which is served to at least three-fourths of the bar diners every Thursday night.

Marcie eats often at Ouest and usually orders the special, which on this Tuesday was a slow-cooked duck with wild rice and various root veggies. I was all fished out from the weekend and steak was on my mind, until I was told that if meat was what I craved and I wanted to test this chef, I should go with the braised short ribs instead. Good choice! Short ribs call for potatoes and parsnips, and the combination is what I had hoped for—with an added dimension of sautéed shiitake mushrooms heaped over the ribs.

The ambience of a friend at the bar to share tastes and stories with is always a treat, and this evening ended with espresso and sweet stories instead of dessert. Where were we? Oh, yes, Ouest, the place I didn't like in the balcony but will come back to in a flash if I am headed for the bar or with friends to one of those great-looking red leather booths!

PAMPANO

209 East 49th Street (2nd and 3rd Avenues) *Zagat: 25*
212-751-4545 *www.modernmexican.com*
Chef: Richard Sandoval

How does this sound: Pastel de Elote—slices of warm corn pudding served with rich coconut ice cream and hibiscus sauce. Eaten at a ten-seat bar with light pouring down from a glass ceiling onto white-on-white walls, bathing your environment with a sun-drenched ambience. Right out of Acapulco? You bet! Right along with celebrity chef Richard Sandoval, who brings you the very upscale version of modern Mexican cuisine, such as a triangle of tacos stuffed with fresh lobster and shrimp in a chipotle sauce with avocado and jicama. And you opera fans and celebrity seekers won't be disappointed if owner Placido Domingo isn't there when you taste this Mexican fare in a setting as different from Mama Mexico and Rosa Mexicano as you can get and still be Mexican.

I couldn't wait to get to the Pampano bar in January to see if that Mexican effect would work on a cold NYC winter's evening. Walking in was warmth itself, and seeing the bar seats almost filled with diners, and another ten unreserved seats in the bar area emitting sounds of delight was what I had hoped for. The Mexican bartender didn't surprise me when he said that margaritas are the most popular cocktail at the bar. There are seven margaritas on the menu, from $11 to $24 for a double to $44 for a suprema. You will find a separate tequila menu, and there are six white wines by the glass from $10 to $13, including a New Zealand sauvignon blanc and a French Sancerre; six reds, including two from Spain and three from Argentina at $10 to $14. Knowing Mexican beers as I do, and loving to have the local beers, I had no trouble choosing one that I had never tasted before, a Noche Buena. I was told that it is a strong, dark lager, one of the tastiest beers from Mexico and made by the same brewery that makes Dos Equis. The name of this beer refers to Christmas Eve, and it has a poinsettia on the label, and yes, it was easily the best, and served without the lime, if you please! (Of course, readers of *Belly Up to the Bar* realize that Corona beer started adding the lime to their beer serving for marketing purposes, not tasting purposes, and those who don't like beer very much love those lime wedges!)

I asked the woman beside me if she had been here before, and followed up with my usual questions about things I most want to know: "Do you eat out often? Do you usually eat at the bar? What are your favorite bars?" Ashley lives in midtown and loves Mexican, travels often to Mexico, and knows more about Mexican food than any of her friends, who usually look down their noses at tacos, enchiladas, and rice and beans. She speaks Spanish and was just finishing what she came for, the seviche tastings ($27 for three pieces—$32 for four) with her margarita. Looking at the menu, I certainly didn't want to try the squid-ink pasta after having it at an Italian restaurant, but I hesitated over the seafood meatballs (an oxymoron?) because I had never seen them on a menu before and they are served in a creamy orange sauce with shavings of truffles. But I wanted to try something familiar with a Sandoval twist, so I ordered the ostiones Pampano for $14, cornmeal-crusted oysters with black bean–mango pico sauce, and a chile chipotle vinaigrette. Those oysters were thrilling with a sauce worthy of a celebrity chef. Ashley thought I made a wise choice. She had gone on to a whole fish for $32 with a side of fried plantains ($5.50), which she ordered so that I would be sure to have a taste of Acapulco from her point of view. "Nothing like the Cuban plantains," she said.

Only one person at the bar was not dining on this cold night at 9:30 when the place was booming with life. An order of lemon-lime flan for $7 should top it all off; even though I didn't want a whole dessert, I figured that my bar neighbor would eat half as I had tasted most of her order. I had come to see if Mexico could rub off in the cold of winter and yes! success was easy. Come to Pampano to warm up to Mexican's best, and check out all of the happy people for yourself.

PAMPLONA

37 East 28th Street (Park and Madison Avenues) *Zagat: 25*
212-213-2328 *www.pamplonanyc.com*
Chef: Alex Ureña

This modern Spanish cuisine earned top rating for Spanish fare in NYC the first year it opened (2006). A husband-wife team, Alex the chef and Martine the manager and host have created a contemporary, serene, intimate environment for serving the best and most innovative Spanish food in town. In 2007, Alex won the Rising Star Chef award with his creative menu.

The Monday night in May I went to check out Pamplona, I found six bar seats, and half of them were taken for dinner at 9:30. I had taken a friend along because we so seldom have a Spanish opportunity other than tapas at Tía Pol, and one can forget having a conversation at Casa Mono because of the noise level, even though the food is at the top of the chain. By 10 p.m. we were almost at the height of the Spanish dinner-time and ready and able to talk over every choice to be made and bite to be appreciated.

The wines by the glass are five whites and seven reds, mostly Spanish wines, and they range in price from $8 to $19. Checking out the appetizers from $15 to $17, we decided to have two, then on to the cheese selections and end with a dessert. Skipping the tapas list, which were $6 each or three for $16, we chose the Maine crabmeat lasagna, mussels, salsa verde for $15, and the roast lamb sausage with chickpea purée, and onion soubise, with a black olive sauce for $15, thinking that the two very different dishes would surely give us a sense of the chef. And different they were! Maine crabmeat is very light and delicate in flavor, and who ever heard of anyone using it for lasagna? My bar pal and I agreed that the presentation itself was worth a visit to Pamplona! Using small white square plates on longer rectangular plates is very effective for such a colorful chef. In the crabmeat dish, we worried a bit that the salsa would be a little too strong—but not to worry, it was a wonderful combination. The lamb sausage was a much heavier dish, and if I had been alone, it would have been just right with a glass of wine for a great supper. As it was, the combination was a treat. The man on my left was having the poached shrimp with a creamy manchego rice and chorizo. He told me that he has had it before, and in fact is a regular and has tried everything. He also said that Alex usually has a daily special in all categories, and most often he just asks for the appetizer, entrée, and dessert chef's specials when he comes to the bar.

The cheese selections were interesting; there were three choices in groups of three, and all were served with pickled pears, quince paste, and olives, which, again, was a first, and don't we adventuresome New Yorkers love firsts? We chose La Peral: three blue cheeses, and your taste buds just can't help but be influenced by the presentation of the small side dishes along with the cheese selection.

All of the desserts are $11, and after much debate we decided to share the white hibiscus and yogurt panna cotta, grapefruit gelée, red hibiscus sauce with cranberry sorbet . . . and red and white it was! Sweet and sour, a wonderful ending to our Spanish evening with Alex, the rising star chef, and Martine, the gracious host, about to give birth to their first child.

PAYARD BISTRO

1032 Lexington Avenue (73rd and 74th Streets) *Zagat: 24*
212-717-5252 *www.payard.com*
Closed: Sundays *Chef: François Payard*

Do you miss Paris? Imagine the most elegant salon de thé, Dalloyau, at the corner of the Luxembourg Gardens and Boulevard Saint Michel—pastries in a glass showcase on the left, handmade chocolates twinned in a showcase on the right, café tables in between as you make your way toward the six bar seats before entering the balconied dining area for the bistro's best. Oh, yes! *Mais oui,* French conversation all around. François Payard, third-generation pastry chef from la belle France, *bien sûr,* and his wife, Alexandra, are very much in view at their joint venture with Daniel Boulud of Restaurant Daniel (Michelin ★★).

"Once they try the bar, they never go back to those stuffy little tables," boasted the continental, young bartender-actor Dana, who graduated from New York City's Lycée, where he learned his French. A white linen napkin, folded in a large triangle, was placed in front of me as I perused the short menu, listened to the beautiful language sounds of the French couple enjoying a drink next to me, and quickly decided on a Sancerre with choices of $10, $11, and $14 a glass (bottles of whites started at $26 and reds at $28, the top of the line being a red Bordeaux, 1999 Grand Cru Classé from Château Valandraud at $950 a bottle). The beers are underappreciated at most French restaurants including this one, which offers Heineken, Budweiser, and the French Fischer, an amber. Payard almost makes up for the ordinary short list, however, because there isn't a more beautiful beer glass in all of New York City than the Fischer beer glass.

Looking at appetizers such as the chilled red beet soup with pickled goat cheese and dill at $10; or the country bread tartine with sardines, green olive tapenade, baked tomatoes, and baby arugula for $12; or the Payard foie gras, which I've often seen others have, at $21, I decided against an appetizer as my eye was on the entrées and desserts. Very pleasing was the miniature apple-picking basket of bread (baguettes) baked on the premises and accompanied by three thick circles of butter, which was enjoyed while watching the people pour into the bistro between 8 and 9 p.m. The café tables were full as patrons sampled the desserts and drank Kir Royals, and one could hear an uncommonly high number of champagne corks popping to go with the unparalleled French pastries. On the dining room side of the bar, a fiftyish, tres, tres chic, exquisitely dressed crowd filled every chair on the ground floor and balcony. The bar attracts all ages, often solos having a dinner, café snack, and many times a dessert and champagne. There are also those at the bar waiting for a table where I have several times seen Alexandra Payard busy making the wait for a table fly by with conversation and attention.

Although tempted by the classic pike quenelles with a shellfish sauce and white truffle oil, I went straight to the steak-frites entrée, a NY sirloin steak with homemade french fries and a four-peppercorn sauce. A traditional bouillabaisse, roasted venison, and a cassoulet were among other choices that were considered. Waiters were bantering *en Française* as they picked up their drink and wine orders for the dining room, French music in the air enlivened the bar atmosphere, and giant martinis with two huge olives each had to be acknowledged as they passed the eye. The smells, energetic sound (a busy, rather than crazy weekend-noise level), and sights were thrilling for Francophiles.

A couple shared a profiterole at the bar with the traditional silver pitcher of hot chocolate poured by the bartender over the cream puff filled with ice cream and slivers of bright orange peel to distract the sight and flavor of the hot fudge. You'll be quickly persuaded that the pastry chef and owner of Payard (the only pastry chef in the United States who is certified by the French Association of Pastry Chefs) is indeed who he says he is by the first taste of his Charlenoit. Just imagine a base of hazelnut-almond meringue with a consistency between that of a soft nut meringue and a sponge cake, soaked with rum syrup. It is spread with chocolate cream and another layer of cake and syrup, then layered with the praline custard cream, about one inch thick. After a layer of cake is added and saturated with rum syrup, it is then decorated on top with a large hazelnut surrounded with pale green marzipan leaves. Topping this bar-dining treasure with an excellent espresso, it was easy to realize that there is no need to miss Paris with Payard in town!

PEARL OYSTER HOUSE

18 Cornelia Street (Bleeker and 4th Streets) *Zagat: 26*
212-691-8211 *www.pearloysterbar.com*
Closed: Sundays *Chef: Rebecca Charles*

I've been to many fish shacks in Maine and on the Cape, and I've been to many in NYC that call themselves fish shacks. But believe me, fish shack doesn't get more fish shack than you'll find at Pearl Oyster! No stage set here . . . maybe Rebecca Charles hired a logging truck from Maine, or a flatbed to haul her fish shack down from Penobscot Bay to Cornelia Street. It's authentic. Finding it is wonderful because being in the Village on Cornelia Street is just what you imagine when thinking Village. When you walk in, you'll see a bar with a dozen seats that comes around the corner, and on the outside wall is a narrower counter with eight more seats. Pearl Oyster has expanded into a tiny dining room, but it's much more fun to find a place at the bar. If you are solo, you'll have a much shorter wait, as there are no reservations for any seat in the house, and being as authentic and as good as it is, you must plan ahead to go early or to work on your patience while waiting for a seat or two.

Beer and wine are the choices you will have to go with your lobster roll or fried oysters. No martinis here. Many choices of microbrews from $7 to $12, and more whites than reds of wine by the glass from $9 to $14. After questioning the waitress about exactly what will be in that famous lobster roll before ordering it to avoid ending up with all kinds of non–New England herbs, I learned that Pearl's oyster roll has only lobster meat, Hellmann's mayo, and a touch of lemon, and is served on a toasted Pepperidge Farm bun. Well, that's exactly what I ordered and that's exactly what I got! Plus the crispy shoestring fries that come with it. They were above par, as well. Must have been those potatoes from Houghton, Maine. I checked out the clam chowder and, once again, no extras: just the cream and milk, clams, potatoes, onions, and in place of salt pork she uses bacon, but that's okay. A northern New Englander wants to know two things about a fish shack—what's the lobster roll like and what's the clam chowder like? If those two plates are in place, you can order anything and count on it being New England authentic.

Down East they have blueberry pie with their lobster, and even though Pearl added her own spin on that pie with a crumble in place of the traditional two-crusted blueberry pie, everyone else seems to like it her way.

Pearl Oyster House is a very friendly place. It's laid-back, and everyone appears happy to be there and getting what they came for. It's open and light; check out the kitchen if you want to—very informal, little shoptalk—all the things that make you feel like you're on a day off when you saunter into the wait line at Pearl Oyster.

PERRY STREET

176 Perry Street (West Street)
212-352-1900

Zagat: 24; Michelin: ★
www.jean-georges.com
Chef: Jean-Georges Vongerichten

Wait until you see Richard Meier's glass tower building in which you will find, on a cobblestoned street looking oh so nonurban, Perry Street restaurant. Wait until you go inside and see, smell, and feel the sophistication of this Jean-Georges modern, minimalist in color and design, big flowers, great village space between everything. There are ten seats at the sleek bar, and another twenty lounge places without reservations in the entrance along the glass walls looking out on the Hudson. At the bar early on a Friday evening, most were just getting started on their cosmopolitans, although one man in his forties was dining at the bar.

Looking forward to many courses that evening at different bars in the West Village, I decided to go for the grilled king oys-

ter mushroom and avocado carpaccio, with charred jalapeño oil and lime, for $14. The rice-cracker-crusted tuna with a citrus emulsion for $17 looked wonderful when I saw it go by to the lounge table by the window. The beer list was better than ordinary with seven bottles, and the Sam Smith Ale was my choice. According to the bartender, there are from ten to twelve wines by the glass, depending on the evening. There are probably as many half bottles ordered as wine by the glass, the bartender added. The one other diner at the bar, Bob, had started with the black pepper dumpling and snow peas, which I had wondered about but decided to wait for Shanghai Pavilion for my crab dumplings.

Bob told me that he always dines at the bar on a Friday night to clear his head from the week, and then goes out with his friends on Saturday nights. His favorites are A Voce and Pampano; both have space between the tables in their main dining rooms so that one can relax without too high a noise level, and he can always plan on excellent food. Craft is next on his list, as I told him that his requirements reminded me of Craft. His choice of the rabbit, which he'd had once before, was prepared as crunchy rabbit, with citrus-chile seasoning and soybean purée, for $31. He has also had the grilled black bass, with ruby grapefruit juice and caramelized radishes, for $28. "Great presentations for all of the entrées," he said. I checked out the desserts, all at $9, and was interested in the oatmeal soufflé, cinnamon apples, and cider sorbet, which I had not seen on a menu before.

You can see, bar diner, that the menu is as modern as the setting—the semicircular banquettes against a wall of glass looking out to the Hudson. Did I say that the seating is white leather, and that the tables are covered with brown-paper place mats and white linen napkins? Very modern lamps add to the MoMA look of Perry Street. It's a long walk back to the subway, so I was glad I started there before moving on to an East Village restaurant for my entrée. Calm and elegant Village comes to mind when thinking of Perry Street. I can see why Bob chose it as his Friday night place to unwind.

PETROSSIAN

182 West 58th Street (7th Avenue) — *Zagat: 24*
212-245-2214 — *www.petrossian.com*
Chef: Michael Lipp

The diners are definitely continental! Straight from Carnegie Hall or Central Park South hotels and residences, there are as many double-breasted suits and coats on the shoulders of the men as one expects to find in Milano or St. Petersburg. One wouldn't be surprised to see men in a Lennie Bernstein–style wool cape at the Petrossian! It is the Russian caviar restaurant, organized to serve caviar and champagne in every form, size, and quality. Housed in a very ornate Renaissance-style building, the Alwyn Court Building, the ambience at NYC's Petrossian resembles that of the Petrossian in Paris. Two brothers founded a company that is tops in importing the best of Russian caviar for both the Paris and New York City restaurants. The caviar prices range from under $100 into the thousands of dollars, depending on amount and type chosen.

This excellent restaurant has a bar the length of the room, with many taking champagne and caviar only, a few with full dinners, and another few with desserts and champagne. Set before us at the bar is a room-length etched Erté mirror in which the sparkling champagne and wine glasses are all reflected from the shelves—the caviar is served only on Limoges china. Lalique crystal wall sconces shine down upon us as we admire the 1930s bronze sculptures. My Carnegie Hall subscriber friend Lita and I ordered a glass of the house champagne, which is La Tour Maubourg, and yes, it was served in a very beautiful champagne flute—the glasses were squeaky sparkly. A white linen square napkin was laid in place with a plate of breads, bread sticks, and rolls with excellent butter.

There is an interesting theater prix fixe for $42 on the menu (as well as one for $68), beginning with smoked salmon with bilini and crème fraîche, and an entrée one could choose included a smoked river trout salad with pickled beets, capers, and egg that looks good. We went with the bilini, as it was a Russian place. We chose the salmon quenelle in Vol-Au-Vent with lobster sauce. The quenelle was on a paper-thin pastry with a dab of caviar on top, served on a forkful of spinach, a sprig of dill on the side, with an excellent lobster sauce. The blend of textures, colors, and flavors easily comes to a 9+.

Our dessert choice was a chocolate torte with raspberry sauce and hazelnut ice cream. The cake was disappointingly much too dry and heavy; two of us couldn't even eat it all, overvalued at a 5! The man next to us had chosen the brown-butter cardamom cake with poached rhubarb and citrus cream. You know how that feels when the other plate looks a lot better than yours! Usually a sign to give more thought to our choices, yes?

A quiet and formal sound and feeling is the ambience presented to the forty- to eighty-plus-year-old patrons. It's no Balthazar! The service couldn't have possibly been better: gracious, attentive, many people catering to everyone's needs in their navy blazers with brass buttons, just like first class shipboard. Most at the bar were enjoying caviar, two oldish men came in after the St. Luke's chorale concert, scores in hand, which they put on the table, and then went over the music while sipping their champagne. Paris? Salzburg? St. Petersburg? Oh, so continental. All at the bar in New York City!

PIANO DUE

151 West 51st Street (6th and 7th Avenues) — *Zagat: 25*
212-399-9400 — *www.pianoduenyc.net*
Closed: Sundays — *Chef: Michael Cetrulo*

Offtrack betting? Oh, no, that's the dramatically dazzling red-and-orange horseracing landmark mural of Sandro Chio, high up toward the ceiling surrounding the complete bar room. There are twenty-one seats around this bar, and the bar is it, with lounge tables hugging the wall around the bar. Michael Cetrulo's formal restaurant is upstairs, by elevator, but as a belly-up-to-the-bar fan, you will want to stay right here at the Palio Bar and enjoy the à la carte menu or have the option of dining on this celebrity chef's tasting menu or full menu.

At 7:30 on a Thursday evening, most were having a drink at the bar or lounge tables, although enough were eating to feel comfortable ordering Michael Cetrulo's signature dish, a soft egg-yolk ravioli stuffed with spinach and ricotta cheese, topped with a taste of black truffle. The relaxed lighting was perfect for conversation, and the bar was completely filled, mostly with men in their forties and fifties, in groups of two or three, who hadn't yet left their workday. The horses racing high above the bar toward a very high ceiling didn't appear to excite the people below. Spirited sports-bar behavior was not de rigueur, business talk at the end of the day was.

I waited about ten minutes for a seat, and ended up beside a couple from Scarsdale who were headed to a Broadway show a few blocks away. Margaret and Jim told me that they come regularly to the Palio Bar before the theater and consider the pretheater dinner a best-kept secret in NYC's theatergoing world. While most of their friends are in honky-tonk tourist places before the theater, they are in this fabulous setting, underneath this landmark racing mural, eating from a Zagat-26-rated chef for a pretheater special at $40! They usually get there by 6 p.m., as the theater special has to be ordered by 6:30, but then they like to leave by 7:30 anyway. Margaret was so eager to tell me how good it was and what they ate that I had to tell the waiter to hold my order, as who wants to eat a cold soft-cooked egg ravioli? With pencil in hand, I wrote as fast as I could to say that they had three choices of a first and second course, plus a dessert, and coffee or tea. I was amused that they were meeting friends at the theater and evidently hadn't even told them about their treasure on Fifty-first!

This Italian chef uses a lot of prosciutto, as you will see. Margaret started with a prosciutto salad with pear, almonds, ricotta, and a citrus-mustard dressing; and Jim had the white bean soup with black truffle raviolini with prosciutto and truffle oil. They agreed that his was the best choice for that evening. He followed with a scaloppini, and she with butterflied shrimp in mustard-basil broth, and they said the entrées were a toss-up, both thrilling tastes. They shared a dessert, and I even got a taste of it, and agreed it was some dessert. There were three chocolate desserts to choose from and six other than chocolate, such as a roasted pineapple dessert, a roasted pear, and caramels and sorbets. Going for the chocolate, they selected the Praline di Giandula, which had layers of baked Italian meringue, hazelnut praline, and dark chocolate ganache, all topped with a drizzle of pistachio cream. I don't know anyone who wouldn't want to top all that with an Italian espresso!

As they hurried out, much later than planned because they loved being informants for *Belly Up to the Bar,* they said not to tell anybody. The bartender told me that many of the tables in the lounge room were the pretheater crowd, and that by 8:30 or 9 p.m. the bar would change from cocktails to bar diners, so at least half would be dining at the bar on weeknights.

PICHOLINE

35 West 64th Street
(Broadway and Central Park West)
212-724-8585

Zagat: 27; Michelin: ★★
www.picholinenyc.com
Chef: Terrance Brennan

If you are in the mood for the best Michelin-starred food in the Lincoln Center area (along with Jean Georges, *bien sûr*)—it's possible to enjoy a dining life of your own at the bar since Picholine's renovation. You will dine at Picholine's bar with a space all your own, and the small lounge tables for all of us without reservations create a wonderful space for this celebrity chef's creations. You can gaze through the bar room into the next two dining rooms with perfect crystal chandelier lighting and beautiful pink-linen walls hung with oil paintings and tapestries. Picholine attracts a beautifully dressed clientele that matches the decor of chef-owner Terry Brennan's Picholine—a French Mediterranean restaurant.

The wine by the glass is more unusual than most, concentrating on smaller, less known vineyards. In fact, one of the wine suppliers sat two bar seats down, reaping his client's good wine selection judgment. Do note, however, all of you not-for-profit school and museum salaried people who love NYC's greatest chefs in spite of your limited resources, there is an $8 and $9 red, and the whites by the glass start at $12, with an excellent beer list that includes Heineken dark as well as light, Sam Smith (from England, not Adams from Boston), and, lucky for me, one of the top ambers, Anchor Steam (the other top ambers are Vermont's Wolover's IPA or Long Trail Ale).

From the new tapas-style menu, you can choose three for $18. The couple on my left were doing just that. The first time I was here with a friend and we considered wild mushroom ox soup, French truffle, scallops with almonds and melon, and sweetbreads. We decided to share the fricassee of Maine oysters with leeks, potatoes, and bacon bits in a vermouth sauce with sprigs of baby parsley on top. The first taste of this creamy vermouth sauce was absolute ambrosia. An honest, solid 10 without a doubt (a very rare occurrence). Little rounds of potato (the leeks were puréed in the sauce), small oysters, and even though my bar pal that evening thought the dish was too small, a 10 is a 10. Next we tasted a second appetizer: organic squash and wild mushroom ravioli with brown butter, walnut, and sage, which was a definite 8. I recently had a 10 on this dish at Gabriel's (11 West Sixtieth Street, Zagat 22), where the sage was blended with the browned butter, rather than a sage leaf on top of the ravioli, and served with less butter. But just you wait for that dessert menu: apple crisp was one option, next a lemon Napoleon, which sounds sacrilegious and horrific to a Francophile. We settled on the pear crêpe with ricotta cheese and Zinfandel syrup. Bingo! Another 10. The standard of excellence. The light crêpe was formed into a cup shape with crisped edges, the peeled roasted pear stood upright on a bed of ricotta cheese, and the Zinfandel syrup of orange and raspberry concentrate circled the plate. Presentation, taste, and texture came together for a perfect dessert. On my second visit in the new space, there were six seats and everyone in the bar was dining instead of just waiting for a seat in the dining room. There were many regulars (not surprising), a great bartender, and very discerning diners thoroughly enjoying everything that they were drinking and eating. An insurance man, Jeff from L.A., was trying the tasting menu of seven courses, and described each one of them as he enjoyed them. The couple on my right wanted to tell me their favorite dining at the bar places, and we loved it because every single one of us were in one conversation . . . top NYC chefs without reservations. Jeff and I were the last ones to leave; he said that he was in NYC for two more nights and wanted suggestions for two more great places at the bar. Having gotten a sense of his taste, I sent him up to Telepan on his second night and for the following evening I thought he should first check out Le Bernardin (he could never get a reservation there and didn't know about the bar) and see if anyone else was eating there, and if not, just keep walking to Columbus Circle and first look in at the Time Warner Building for Porter House New York, then check out Café Grey, and go with whichever followed his mood. Jeff said he could hardly wait to get through tomorrow's business in order to give that strategy a try! With the emphasis now on a room of our own, that is, diners at Picholine's bar without reservations, I just can't wait to go back!

PORTER HOUSE NEW YORK

10 Columbus Circle (Time Warner Center),
Fourth Floor
212-823-9500

Zagat: 22
www.porterhousenewyork.com
Chef: Michael Lomonaco

A New York City big-time steak house in the most dramatic scene at the Time Warner Center, Columbus Circle, is, as you will expect, filled with men seeking their dry-aged prime beef and seafood. Popular is an understatement, even though it just opened in the spring of '07; the reasonable prices compared to Café Gray, Per Se, and Masa in the same center are not to be discounted.

Designed for plenty of bar room with a magnificent view of Central Park, there are thirteen seats at the main bar as you enter the restaurant, and in addition there are twelve seats at high tables with bar seats in the bar area, plus four more before entering the restaurant section. I went to Porter House on a midweek evening at 8:30, wanting to be sure to see the diners at the bar. There were many thirties and forties men on hand among the fifties and sixties; business dress is the common look that one expects to see at Time Warner, and a few women with briefcases in business attire were in the groups of three or four men standing as well as sitting at the bar. The bartender told me that the number of regulars for dinner was beyond any other restaurant at which he has worked.

A traditional steak-house fare is exactly what is offered, with oysters to start at $3 each, shrimp cocktail, crab cakes, and salads including a field greens for $10. The aged, prime T-bone is $42, and the menu includes veal and lamb chops as well at $41 and $38; the usual Maine Lobster is offered at $42, some classic sauces, and listen to these sides for $9: macaroni and cheese with four cheeses, buttermilk onion rings, spinach two ways, roasted beets with mustard seed and dill, pan-roasted mushrooms, and six kinds of potatoes including creamy gratin. See what I mean? Men's comfort food.

Now here is an added dimension of this steak house at the Time Warner Center: a nightly special that changes often. The week I was there it started out on Monday night with calves' liver, bacon, and caramelized onions for $23, building up to Thursday night Aurora Cowboy rib steak for $56, and including

NY strip steak on Tuesday, filet-mignon tips for $29 on Wednesday, braised short ribs for $31 on Friday night, veal osso buco with saffron risotto on Saturday night for $37, and chicken pot pie on Sunday night at $22.

I sat at the bar with a restaurateur from San Francisco checking out how things work in the Big Apple, who was sampling as many menu items as he could, including several of the

sides. I didn't feel like filet-mignon tips, the nightly special, and so I tried the seared sea scallops at $18, which were really good with capers, brown butter, and crisp parsley. I just loved it! Almost as much as butternut squash ravioli in brown butter and sage. I followed that with a side of sautéed garlic spinach and polenta with porcini mushrooms at $14. I know, a funny mix, but why go to the bar if you can't have lopsided meals? Besides that, these three things weren't on Fred's list, the San Francisco guy, and we discussed what I was ordering with that in mind. By 10:30 the buzz was a happy one in as NYC a steak house as you would ever want in midtown. And remember this, the price is right for where you are!

PRUNE

54 East 1st Street (1st and 2nd Avenues) *Zagat: 24*
212-677-6221 *www.prunerestaurant.com*
Chef: Gabrielle Hamilton

Looking for real East Village? Well, not too real, but authentic East Village? Come to this little hole-in-the-wall restaurant with a noise level that will make up for the stature of the place. Voices bouncing off the tile floor aren't the whole story; some kind of beat was coming from a loud music system that made the background complete. The tiny bar matches the tiny restaurant, a zinc, not much more than ten inches wide, with four wooden seats to sample Gabrielle's (chef-owner) creative, seasonal, very fine cuisine.

Starting with sorrel soup (a first), I was told that the sorrel arrived just as I was sitting down. It was puréed in a chicken broth, cream and lemon juice added, with a dollop of crème fraîche. Yummy is an understatement. The beer list included a Belgian, French, British, and two American beers, and I was pleased to see a Kronenbourg 1664 on the list for $7. There are five reds and five whites by the glass from $7 to $13, and a couple of sparkling wines were on the list as well. On the counter with the beer came a little dish of fried (in oil and salted) chickpeas, which were light and delightful. Asking for bread was the right thing to do . . . it was remarkable bread, nice and crusty on the outside with air bubbles on the inside. You will have to ask for the butter, but it will be worth it because that was top butter on fab bread.

Just as I was starting the soup, a couple from Calgary joined me at the bar, first trip to New York City and they had never dined at the bar (couldn't get reservations at the top places—of course we New Yorkers knew that). That added a lot more tastes to my evening. They tasted the sorrel soup and ordered a special Italian cheese on toast for a first course (it appeared like mozzarella, but it tasted much more like a specialty). I went on to an artichoke with brown butter for $9 with a glass of French Sancerre for $11, and then they ordered the roasted marrow bones for $14 and the stewed pork shoulder for $24, which they had never had, and had been told to order here at Prune.

The menu lists things in any order, so that there are no "Appetizers," "Entrées," and "Sides" distinctions to consider. The steak is $29. Just guess by the price what size the plate will be. And of course the better to order as lopsided a dinner as you want. I decided to try the panna cotta after my soup and veggie. I had only had it once before—a perfect panna cotta at Lupa. This one was topped with blueberries, and, lucky me, even with high expectations it was delightfully light, perfect texture, and a not-too-sweet end to the evening. My Calgary neighbors had never tasted panna cotta before, so with extra spoons that turned out well, too. The Calgary couple was in NYC for an international lawyers meeting for three nights. This was their first foray into the top chefs, Babbo was their second evening's plan, and they were going to ask around for a third. If you can stand the heat of the kitchen and the noise of the dining room, you'll love the home-style (don't we wish our own home-style was this creative?) of Gabrielle's cuisine.

PUBLIC

210 Elizabeth Street (Prince and Spring Streets) *Zagat: 23*
212-343-7011 *www.public-nyc.com*
Chef: Brad Farmerie

Grilled kangaroo, anyone? On a coriander falafel with lemon-tahini and green pepper relish for $14? How's that for a Down Under Pacific sound? Heading for the Tasting Room (a Zagat 22), I couldn't resist going into the Public; the fact that it is billed as an Aussie restaurant peaked my interest, since I have a daughter living in New Zealand and a best friend in Sydney. What a treat! A great-looking bar with fourteen seats, and every seat taken this early in the evening. A wine tasting room, a dining room, all kinds of space in Brad Farmerie's place. Brad is a Pittsburgh-born and -raised chef who has learned his trade all over the world. I was given a great tour by friendly and gracious Australian Christina O'Neil, who showed me around, explained the expertise, and showed off the chef's awards on this busy night at the Public. My guess was that the Public meant the UK pub, but no, it represents salvaged pieces from public spaces and buildings. Library shelves, for example, post office boxes, and public antiques and collectibles, make it look the age of its original building, which was a muffin factory in Nolita.

I was just passing by and planned to dine at another bar, but still, I didn't resist just one Foster's to toast my Down Under family and friends, and to check out the menu and try the wild boar that I spotted on the menu as a starter. Some starter! It was served with garrotxa cheese, marinated olives, and capers for $14. Hmmm, a little gamey, more like wild Vermont venison than moose or caribou, for example. I'll admit, I'll try anything once, although I'm a fast learner and don't always try everything twice.

I sat near Ian, a young Aussie bloke who was talking the talk and going to eat later. He told me that he is a regular and usually goes for the Tasmanian sea trout ($25) when he feels like fish, and for the New Zealand venison with cabrales dumplings, mushrooms, and salsa verde ($27.50) when he feels like meat. He hadn't yet tried the wild boar, and never eats kangaroo—"Just for the tourist," said Ian. He says that he feels at home at Public, and that he has never been there when it wasn't a happy place to be with a major male crowd in their thirties and forties, and always, always a few from Down Under. "You'd be surprised at how many Kiwis and Aussies there are in NYC—we all travel a year or two when we finish school, and it used to be only to the UK, but now as many come to the USA." I guess I am not surprised and have even learned to tell the difference between the New Zealand and Australian accents, which is no easy task for an American. Moving on after the red Australian wine that the bartender said I must have as the Foster's just won't hold up to the game, I left promising I'd be back to show off this chef and restaurant to friends.

RAOUL'S

180 Prince Street (Sullivan and Thompson Streets) — *Zagat: 24*
212-966-3518 — *www.raouls.com*
Chef: David Honeysett

Funk? You thought you knew funk? Wait until you sit at one of these dozen bar seats and look up at the stuffed antlered deer—not even looking straight at you, but with its head turned right and looking right toward the spiral staircase leading to the only restrooms! And beside the deer, an "easy read" school clock to keep you timed to your task. And above all of that, a pressed tin ceiling circa 1850s. Not a whole lot of oldish people in the restaurant—mostly a loud and noisy group in their thirties and forties. Oh! Here comes a couple over sixty; they are regulars and so of course they know about that open spiral staircase. And Norman, another regular, who is proudly eighty-seven years old, came in around 9 p.m., as promised by the bartender.

The layout of this fab French bistro cuisine with a 24 rating is something to come to look at. Oil paintings across from the bar wall, leading out to the configuration of a few booths and other tables, leading out to the kitchen, through which you must go as the chefs step closer to their stoves and work counters to let you pass to the garden room! Funk is fun without question at Raoul's, a thriving thirty-three-year-old survivor of NYC Soho restaurants.

Raoul's has a friendly bartender who is attentive and eager to describe the menu and beers and wines. There were at least ten different bottled beers, including a few French, and a Fisher, amber, the best of the lot. Bar-pal Helen found standing room near those spiral stairs to have a glass of Merlot while we waited about ten minutes for two seats at the bar on a Monday night in September around 8 p.m. By 9 p.m. eight of the twelve were dining at the bar. The appetizers run from $9 to $145 for a caviar and byline dish. That's kind of funky right there: $9 to $9 to $9 to $11 to $145! Helen ordered a butternut squash risotto, kale, and wild mushrooms; I ordered the house pâté with spinach, olives, and toast triangles. The spinach and olives were better than the pâté, and the risotto was excellent! The entrées ranged from $18 to the saddle of lamb for $39. We decided to share the Margret. (We asked, "Is that duck?" "Yes, breast of duck, a special duck raised especially for fois gras.") We should have realized when we saw steak knives coming with the duck, even though it was perfectly rare—as ordered—and divided in the kitchen and served on an exquisite cherry sauce, it had to have been the toughest duck that either of us had ever put in our mouths! Desserts were $8 to $9 with a warm chocolate cake with hazelnut ice cream, crème brûlée, banana bread pudding, profiterole, fig in port wine with almond ice cream, and we chose the poached pear tart with pear sorbet and crème fraîche. New Yorkers have loved this so-called Parisian setting for years. I agree, it's one of a kind and very friendly, with a marvelous menu . . . come on down, but order the renowned steak au poivre to go with those steak knives!

RED CAT

227 10th Avenue (23rd and 24th Avenues)
212-242-1122

Zagat: 24
www.theredcat.com
Chef: Jimmy Bradley

Eric took the train over from Penn to see what we could see and taste in Chelsea at the bar. We met at Red Cat because we wanted to have our entrée there and go on to check out Cookshop for dessert and coffee. I decided to start earlier and do an appetizer at Buddakan before we met because the chef had come from Philadelphia and Eric already knew all about him. And that's the way we did it on that warm, spring evening. Eric arrived first and saved me a place at the twelve-seat bar, which was filled when I arrived at 6:40! A woven tweed plastic place mat was put before us and a drinks menu with nine beers between $6 and $10; nine white and seven red wines by the glass from $8 to $18. Unlike any other list I'd seen, both the beers and wines were arranged from light to dark, or to full-bodied. I decided to go for a sauvignon blanc for $11, and Eric had a cabernet sauvignon from the Shafer winery because he had visited the winery last summer on a bicycle trip through the Napa Valley. The bartender was all business, and as there were radishes on the bar as snack food, I was thinking French, but when I asked for butter, as the French always serve butter with radishes, he couldn't imagine why I wanted butter. Eric and I thought he was the most antisocial bartender we had met to date. But we loved the menu! And Eric loved his memories of the Napa Valley as he sipped his Cabernet. In fact he told me that it tasted like cassis, chocolate, tobacco, espresso, and licorice all rolled into one! Oh boy . . . I'm for that!

Lots of regulars at the bar at that hour who knew where to get the good food. The wood paneling and bar, the wall lamps with red shades, the brass lanterns hanging down over the bar, all create a cozy look; while the red plates and white linens with contemporary art give the restaurant a very sophisticated look, which draws the Chelsea art gallery crowd. A cosmopolitan art and gay scene, although there were enough informally dressed people there for everyone to feel comfortable. Many couples at the bar, mostly in their forties and fifties.

Checking out the appetizers, Eric chose the beet tartare with chèvre and pine nut oil for $12, and I never can resist the Brandade de Morue with kalamata olives for $11 whenever I see it on the menu, which is seldom. You may know this dish, it's kind of a French shepherd's pie, starting with mashed potatoes, but instead of lamb it's cod and lots of garlic. Brandade is a terrific starter if it's a small enough portion, and it's a wonderful Sunday night supper by itself. Even though I didn't want to taste that chèvre on the beet tartare, Eric reminded me that most people love it, and so to be sure to mention what a great combination it is at the Red Cat!

Moving on to the entrées, I had the crispy skate wing for $21, and Eric enjoyed his sautéed duck breast with scallion wild-rice cakes, wilted greens, and a mango red wine sauce for $28. We were both very impressed with our choices—the presentation and combinations served were certainly up to their rating. We talked our heads off about college admissions and the retirement of the dean of admissions of twenty years at Penn, and how competitive these days are for high school students and their families. But we also enjoyed our surroundings in Chelsea and this Red Cat experience. I'm hoping for a happier bartender next time, but outside of that, the size of the bar and the friendliness of everyone at it assure a return trip.

SAN PIETRO

18 East 54th Street (5th and Madison Avenues) *Zagat: 24*
212-753-9015 *www.sanpietro.net*
Closed: Sundays *Chef: Antonio Bruno*

Elegant setting. The Bruno brothers are from Campania in southern Italy, and the entrance shows the ceramics, paintings, and other artwork from throughout their beloved region. According to Antonio, they proudly import 85 percent of the ingredients from his Italian homeland, which he uses to ensure authentic southern Italian. The seven padded bar seats with backs are very comfortable and usually occupied by single regulars. It's a quiet, older crowd in this wonderful, classical room with paintings; a small, warm, very upscale midtown luxury Italian look. "They say" that regulars are treated better here than newcomers, but the beauty of the bar is that bartenders tend to be less formal and welcome everyone to their little territory. San Pietro is known for feeding Italian diplomats, authors who write about Italy, and Italian businessmen, and you will soon see that a tie to Italy will get you the best seats in the house. Lucky me, I didn't have to give my non-Italian name to anyone on the phone to get my seat at the bar!

The wine list is renowned for representing the largest cellar of southern Italian wines in NYC, as well as wines from all over the world. There are about sixteen wines by the glass, which vary with the season, as does the restaurant's wine cellar. They pride themselves on wines from ancient grapes, drinking wines that the Romans drank and that bring a heritage connecting history with today's San Pietro.

As you look at the menu, keep in mind that you are coming for classical and traditional Italian, with authentic rather than creative in the mind of the chef. The starters range in price from $14 to $20 and include a beef carpaccio with grilled zucchini, lemon juice, and olive oil for $18; and the capanata for $16. The risotto ranges in price from $25 to $26, the fish from $32 to $35, the chicken from $28 to $30, and the meats up to $38 for the T-bone steak. Sides such as salads and vegetables are from $12 to $16. The pastas on the menu in the spring ran from $22 to $26, and I was tempted to try the classic pasta dish of the chef, spaghetti with fresh cherry tomatoes and basil, for $23, but went instead for the dish that Antonio brought to America, first on his menu, linguini with the juice of anchovies, lemon, garlic, and olive oil for $23. And yes, it was perfection! The pasta exactly right, the olive oil of the very best quality, and a wonderful balance of flavors with the whisper of anchovy.

The bartender filled me in on the regulars, mostly midtown finance guys who love simple Italian that comforts rather than confuses them. They don't want to think about their food on the one hand, but want the best on the other. It appears that is exactly what they get from Chef Antonio Bruno in this very serene, calm, classy, luxurious dining room.

SHANGHAI PAVILION

1387 3rd Avenue (78th and 79th Streets) *Zagat: 22*
212-585-3388

Chef: Zong-Xin-Tu

Been to Joe's Shanghai for those crab-pork soup dumplings? Don't feel like going way down to Chinatown? These best-in-the-United-States dumplings are served right on the Upper East Side, and I've even met Upper West Siders who have come over to the East Side in spite of the politics just for this treat. The decor is modern black and red with a lot of brick; a very comfortable, welcoming dining bar as you enter the first dining room, and another dining room toward the back, although it is a small restaurant as Chinese restaurants go. I often go to the bar just for the dumplings, steamed and served in their bamboo steamers; there are six to savor. If you take a pal to the bar with you, you can go on to something else.

Many dishes at this upscale Chinese to match the neighborhood market must be ordered a day ahead, as they specialize in Chinese banquet meals with dishes such as their best-known beggar's chicken, which consists of a chicken stuffed with pork and vegetables, cooked in a clay pot for a day with ginger and rice wine. And the other most-talked-about dish to order a day ahead is the duck with eight treasures, which is stuffed with chicken, scallops, ham, and mushrooms among other things for $36. But back to the three upholstered bar seats and the famous dumplings brought in by this chef from his previous work at Joe's Shanghai in Queens. I first tasted these soup crab and pork dumplings at the Joe's Shanghai in their Chinatown restaurant, and there is no way in the world that I can forget them. I have even gone down to Chinatown before the Pavilion arrived uptown, ordered only the soup dumplings, and bartered half of them away with anyone at the table who had other things that looked interesting. Six of them are a lot to eat for this bar diner.

What must be spelled out here, though, is how to eat soup dumplings. They are always served with a spoon—you know, those Chinese soup spoons? And if you try to pick up one of the very delicate, tulip-shaped and twisted-at-the-end dumplings with your chopsticks and the soup dribbles out before you catch it, then you've lost the whole point of this outstanding dish. So here's the secret. Somehow get the dumpling carefully onto your spoon. Now take your chopstick in the other hand and carefully prick a small hole into it before lifting it off the spoon so that you catch all of the soup and sip and savor it from the spoon, giving full attention to that flavor of crab mixed with pork, and then you pop the dumpling into your mouth. Have a sip of your Chinese beer, and you'll see, you'll be in Chinese heaven! Hey! Not only Tsingtao from China, you can also have Supporo from Japan or Tiger from Singapore for $6. Ahhh, just writing about it makes me want to stop everything I'm doing and get to one of those Zong-Xin-Tu soup dumplings.

What else? Well, there is a whole menu with items such as bean curd dishes, as light and delicious as you'll find anywhere—a bean curd topped with crab and sauced with ginger for $12, as well as a pan-fried curd in the chef's special sauces. Did I say that those soup dumplings are $7? I have ordered a day ahead and been with a group of colleagues to enjoy most of the menu, but it's belly up to the bar for a gourmet snack when I'm on my way somewhere else for the sight and smell of that round bamboo steamer for which I most often go to Shanghai Pavilion.

SHUN LEE WEST

43 West 65th Street
(Columbus and Central Park West)
212-595-8895

Zagat: 23
www.shunleewest.com
Chef: Man-Sun-Do

It's perfect! You forgot to make reservations before Lincoln Center. You worked late, you have to meet your friends, and you're starved! Or you've just come out of a late Lincoln Plaza movie and you are craving a bite at this time of night! Make your way to the bar at Shun Lee West. Not the Shun Lee Café, which isn't as good, but the bar with a menu for the real, Hollywood version of a Chinese restaurant with celebs abounding, a red-and-black-lacquered-decor kind of place. It's another world in the main dining room with dragons overhead. But you are going to be in the lounge area between the main restaurant and café, both of which are packed most of the time with people who order very traditional Chinese food. And you are going for a quick bite in the Lincoln Center neighborhood of very, very good bites and tastes, and even more if you have the time.

The times when I've dined at the bar have almost always been before a Lincoln Center performance, and the bar usually has a seat or two free of their nine seats. A lot of martinis flow out from the bar, and there are a few beers other than Chinese Tsingtao, which I always like to get just on principle of keeping to the culture.

When I've been at this bar with a friend, we usually get the grilled scallops for $14.95 and the crispy shrimp balls at the same price. The list of appetizers starts at $7.75 for the scallion pancakes to a high of $17.95 for BBQ spare ribs or for the honey baby back ribs. There is also an excellent cold appetizer, a duck with Hunan sauce, for $15.95. When I've been solo and not sharing, I like to get the Szechuan bouillabaisse, the seafood and fish slices in a tangy, spicy fish broth for $11.95. I have noticed that many of the martini drinkers go for the ribs, and also for the shrimp. The menu is a long one with all kinds of chicken, pork, and fish choices. The Shun Lee West bar is not as much a destination spot for creative and innovative ways to do Chinese tasting as it is a bar of convenience where you will find superb traditional Chinese food on your way to or from your performance in a very special setting.

SPIGOLO

1561 2nd Avenue (81st Street) *Zagat: 25*
212-744-1100

Chefs: Scott and Heather Fratangelo

Call a year ahead if you want to get a table at this tiny (thirty-four seats including six at the bar), top-of-the-ratings, northern Italian restaurant opened on the Upper East Side in 2005. In summer, we get a break with outdoor tables, which line the sidewalk in the front and on the side of the restaurant. Just like the bar, these seats are without reservations, and lucky for a very few of us, the bar is always without reservations. Mostly a neighborhood crowd who didn't take long to get used to dining on Scott and Heather's northern Italian cuisine in a cheerful restaurant (even the Metropolitan Museum execs count this Second Avenue treasure as "neighborhood"). Scott is working away in the kitchen while Heather does a great job as friendly host, describing dishes in the detail that foodies relish, remembering names as if everyone was an old friend, and doing all of this PR work after spending the early hours in the kitchen on the desserts, as she is the superb pastry chef.

Scott and Heather worked together at Union Square Café, so you can be sure they both know what they are doing and didn't get into their jobs by whim, but through the hard work of learning the trade among chefs with the highest standards. In the three times that I have dined at Spigolo, I have found a seat if I arrived by 7 p.m. at the nice, wide, all-copper bar with friendly Scottie (not to be confused with chef Scott), who knows her menu well. This would be true no matter what night of the week we are talking about, although I wouldn't even guess what the waiting time would be like in summer when I'm out of town.

The beer selection has expanded from the nothing to brag about with Bud, Heineken, and Beck's Dark to now include Anchor Steam, Bass Ale, and a nonalcoholic beer. There are wines by the glass, ranging from seven whites at $11 to $14, seven reds from $9 to $17 for a Chianti Classico, a Persecco for $11, and two rosés. Oysters on the half shell are as fresh, cool, and briny as I had imagined them to be. My second visit, I went for an antipasti and dessert and tried a signature dish that is always on the tasting menu of braised octopus with tomato, chilies, and garlic crostini for $10.

Jeff, my colleague and bar-research pal, opened the evening with a white wine and the trofie with wild mushrooms and pecorino Romano for $13. It's hard to be in a Zagat-25 Italian restaurant and not taste their polenta. We agreed that we could still have dessert and taste the creamy polenta with fontina. Of course we both tasted the octopus, the trofie, and the polenta, and nothing was a bit disappointing! The entrées are from $24 to $29 and include a dish that I'd had before—the fettuccine with lamb ragu, pine nuts, olives, and mint. Also worth talking about is the breast of veal with pancetta, butternut squash purée, and braised escarole. But we were right on to the dessert after the anipasti and a shared primi with polenta.

Recently, I just had to stop by to try the signature dish of sheep milk ricotta gnocchi with pancetta and radicchio. I had them hold the pancetta, and I have to say that if anyone has tasted lighter, creamier, perfectly blended herbed sauced gnocchi with that rich sheep cheese, I'd hold them to a juried trial!

The noise level in winter is high, although it's a happy high with thirties to over fifties enjoying being out in a friendly favorite place. In summer, the French doors are open wide and noise can just fly out the window and up to the sky. My third visit was with two friends, and so of course we didn't hit the bar with three, but got a sidewalk table. The menu was right up there to the usual standard, and when I checked out the bar, all six seats were taken by diners.

Spigolo is a place to go for the food. If you are on the Upper East Side without a reservation, you're in for a treat. Scott and Heather are to be congratulated; they now have their dreams in hand—a new restaurant and a new baby girl.

STRIP HOUSE

13 East 12th Street (5th and University Avenues) *Zagat: 25*
212-328-0000 *www.theglazиergroup.com*
Chef: John Schenk

Well, it's fun to walk into the red lighting and red-flocked wallpaper at Strip House after going to some foreign French film across the street at Cinema Village on Thirteenth. Besides the faux sexy lighting and ambience are the red leather banquettes and black-and-white photos of famous strippers of long ago. But the warm greeting from a recent Marymount College grad, and the smell of those prime, dry-aged New York strip steaks (the signature entrée with both single and double cuts—$40 for the sixteen-ounce), soon pulls your mind to the menu. Strip House has a filet mignon at $34 for the ten-ounce, and the bartender told me that on some nights the filet mignon is served as a special with foie gras and truffle shavings, that it's the hit of the week for many of the regulars at the bar.

There are twelve seats at the bar, and on a Tuesday night around 8 p.m. there were four young women dining there, just so you know that it isn't a men-only feeling at this steak house. In addition to the unreserved bar seats are four tables in the lounge area, with four seats at each table and usually without reservations, although on this particular Tuesday night in June, and in some other nights with a full house, they are reserved.

The appetizers start at $11 for a green salad to $17 for jumbo shrimp. But I couldn't wait to try the lamb shank and cabbage flan for $14. This was served with roasted garlic cloves (and of course everyone knows how great they taste on crusty bread), mushrooms, and a rosemary sauce. Much more creative than the traditional NY steak house. Who ever heard of such a thing? Strip House also does the usual steak-house menu, although the proverbial creamed spinach has a black truffle cream—$10, and the potatoes are fried in goose fat—$10.

Mostly a thirties and forties crowd, mostly in couples, rather than a "boys' night out," which you may think from the restaurant's name. On the dessert menu you will find a share size for both the Strip House cheesecake ($14) and the Strip

House chocolate cake ($16). No one at the bar was tempted, but I spied the cheesecake in the center of a table near the bar where everyone was digging in with very happy looks on their faces. If you are in the neighborhood by yourself after a movie, or you take a friend, you will have to smile when you step into Strip House.

SUEÑOS

311 West 17th Street (8th and 9th Avenues) *Zagat: 23*
212-243-1333 *www.suenosnyc.com*
Chef: Sue Torres

A hot spot in Chelsea that chef-owner Sue Torres created, Sueños is a warm, wonderfully Mexican-colored restaurant. Very informal with a festive look, sound, and taste with reds: magenta, fuchsia, orange, yellow colors, and red leather booths looking out on a glassed-in room onto a sculptured natural garden. The bar has a dozen seats, many young friends gathered around, most of them dining at the bar, more of them dining with a margarita than not, everyone there for one of the best in Mexican. There are counters and bar seats along the outer walls as well as at the bar, which leads into the main dining room. Come on a Sunday or Tuesday night and you can get a Make Your Own Tacos and Tostadas special at $35 a person. That would be hard to do at the bar, but you might want to come back with a gang of friends after you try this bar.

Let's start with all of those beers! There are seven beers on draught, including Dos Equis at $6, and seven more bottles, also at $6, which include one of my favorites, Negra Modelo. If I had been anywhere else I would have tried the Stoudt's Scarlet Lady on draught, a Pennsylvania brewery that wins many awards, but in a Mexican restaurant? Not for me tonight. But of course most are drinking margaritas, with many choices from $9 to $49. The wine list is a long one, and you will have a chance at this bar to order wine by the glass or even the half glass. There are eight whites ranging from $6.75 to $11, with half glasses beginning at $3.50 for both red and white. There are also eight reds from $7 to $14.

I've been back a few times to double-check if it is always such a festive scene, and *sí!* It is! There is a prix-fixe menu with three courses from 5 to 7 p.m. every night for $30. But for most of us, we will enjoy choosing from this fascinating menu with at least ten appetizers at $8 to $12, eleven main courses from $16 to $24, and six desserts ranging from $7 to $9. On the last evening I was there, I decided to skip the appetizer and go for a main course. I decided that I would like the new experience of matching my beer with a main course prepared with the same beer. And so I ordered the chile-rubbed goat wrapped in banana leaf and steamed in Negra Modelo for $24. I loved it! And I liked the idea of having goat in this Mexican setting. I only wish my son had been with me; he lives in Puerto Rico and would relish this dish and eat half of it. Well, when I said all of that out loud, the woman next to me said she had never tasted goat and she would like to try. Aha . . . Now I was all set, I could order a dessert. Mango was on my mind, so I had a few tastes of the guava-and-cream-cheese empanadas with mango coulis.

After comparing Sueños with Crema and Pampano, my bar neighbor and I decided that all three Mexican restaurants were so different that we couldn't compare. Pampano is much more highbrow with fewer Mexicans eating there. Crema doesn't feel as Mexican, and Sueños has a lot of young Latino women at the bar, not found at the other two bars. We liked them all for different moods and reasons. I left this bright spot with several friends in mind to bring with me next time.

SUSHI OF GARI

402 East 78th Street (1st and York Avenues) *Zagat: 26; Michelin:* ★
212-517-5340 *www.sushiofgari.com*
Closed: Mondays *Chef: Gari Sugio*

If Michelin is your restaurant guide to the food world, then you should know that Sushi of Gari is one of three Japanese restaurants with a Michelin star. Karuma Zushi also has one star, and Masa has two. And that's it! If the word on the street is your guide, then Sushi of Gari is the number one Japanese sushi restaurant in New York City. If your own experience is your guide, then I can't wait until you visit this superb Japanese restaurant and send me an e-mail with your review (BellyUpToBarNYC@aol.com). Take the #6 train to Seventy-seventh Street, walk across Seventy-eighth Street until you come to First Avenue, and just across First toward York you'll see a blue awning leading to the entrance of an unobtrusive small restaurant. Walk inside (keep in mind that it's closed on Mondays; I want to be the only one making that mistake), and you will see plain and simple. Brick walls with lamps on the walls, long banquettes on each side with single wooden chairs across from tables in front of the banquettes for the length of the small space. All of these chairs are reserved far in advance, but it's dining with Gari without reservations at the fourteen seats surrounding the master's bar and workspace that you are after.

The second time I visited, there was a fortysomething man on my left who lives next door to the restaurant and comes in whenever he can part with about $85 for dinner as he always goes for the omakase. "I never order. I put myself in the master's hands and just can't imagine more exquisite tastes. My wife does the flowers around the trees along this street, and we reward ourselves for good deeds by taking turns coming here for sushi. We haven't yet both eaten here at the same time. But we're young and look forward to that experience." Looking around, there are solos at the bar, but many couples, and more than half are Asians.

Starting right off by deciding that I didn't begin to know enough about choosing the particular fishes that are flown in daily from Japan, I decided I'd better follow the neighbor's example and learn from the omakase. In this case, that meant a lot of learning, because the staff was very eager for their diner to know everything that goes into the sushi, and in what order it should be served and eaten, and you don't get the next taste until you have admired and savored the sushi of the moment. I was first served the tuna tartare special, and it was explained that this is the belly from the bluefin, not the ordinary yellowfin. I am going to take it that the waiter realized he needed to tell me that difference.

The offerings are different each day, depending on the fresh fish at hand, and so I am going to mention only two particularly unforgettable forever and ever tastes that I encountered. And before going, if you are going to have the attention that you will get at Gari's place, you may want to brush up on how to eat sushi on page 139, so that you won't insult the master by putting your wasabi into the soy. Oh, yes! The unforgettables were the torched yari-squid with creamy sea urchin sauce.

Watching Gari, you will notice that he often uses a blowtorch to get the singe and flavors he is after. The other remember-forever was the shabu-shabu, a snow crab with yuzu sauce. I didn't think I could possibly have any more, even though I ate as slowly and thoughtfully as I was instructed, but when the tempura-fried ice cream with rhubarb sauce arrived, I did manage a couple of bites. Just think of the many times in the city when you spent $85 and it wasn't the best in the world! I can promise you that you'll love spending your money at Sushi of Gari.

TABLA

11 Madison Avenue (25th Street)
212-889-0667

Zagat: 25
www.tablany.com
Chef: Floyd Cardoz

You won't have to climb the suspended stairs to the mezzanine restaurant when you're headed for the ground-floor bread bar at another of Danny Meyer's top-of-the-line restaurants, this kind of American, kind of Indian, feels more like Indian to an American.

There was an awful lot of hype when Tabla opened, and many of us rushed to be one of the first to try it out. My quick pace was slowed down when I walked across the threshold and took one whiff, and then a great inhale of the most comforting food smell in the world—the smell of bread baking, and in this case, bread with all of those sensuous Indian accents along with it. Of course bar diners at NYC's best are very aware of smell when they enter a restaurant. Maybe unconsciously. Now that you think of it, make a habit of smelling, rather than focusing on the look, the minute you enter a restaurant. When I smell good food is when I love to be there. When I smell the carpet is when I turn around and try somewhere else. Bring that sense of smell to the front lobes of your brain and consciousness so that you add another vital dimension to your dining experience—and if you haven't practiced it before, this is the perfect training ground for your sense of smell. Where are we? Oh, yes, belly up to the bar at Tabla!

There are twelve seats at the bar, and you are going to love the beer list! You can count on six draughts and nine bottles from all over the world, priced from $6 to $32 for a 750 ml Dogfish Head 90-Minute IPA. I chose the draught of this Dogfish IPA for $7.50. If bitter IPAs are your thing, you are going to love Dogfish Head! An Indian beer? There is one—Maharaja for $7. For the wine drinkers, you will find a selection of seven whites and six reds from $8 to $17, and also fourteen half bottles.

And now let's get right to the tandoori breads: You can have a naan cheddar cheese and red pepper for $8, a naan sourdough with smoked bacon for $11, or you can go with the selections at $4 to include the mustard seed garlic corn bread, the roasted garlic bread, and the sourdough and sea salt. I had tried the corn bread and the roasted garlic on my first trip here, and this time added the sourdough and sea salt. Looking at the menu by starters, vegetables, seafood, and meat, the beauty of this bar dining is that you can go for bread and beer, or add one of these courses, or all of them.

On the early evening that I was there in November, I decided to forgo the onion rings, crisped in chickpeas flour, cornmeal, and pepper for $11 because everyone else around me had those. So I thought I'd try the chickpea masala with pomegranate seeds and mango powder at $9. So easy to spread on that roasted garlic bread.

The fiftyish man beside me and I started a conversation about dining at the bar. Steve, who lives near Madison Park and often has dinner at this bar, was having a curry of lamb meatballs cooked with dry ginger, fennel seeds, and yogurt for $19, which I can imagine is a new taste in the popular meatball recipes this season. I decided on the striped bass seviche for $12 after all of that bread. Steve said that besides the usual best dining bars of Danny Meyer—although he seldom goes next door to Madison Eleven because it's always so noisy and crowded—he likes Pampano best. Well, we know these bars . . . we noisy people like Eleven Madison, we Mexican-vacation-in-the-sun people like Pampano, and we smellers love Tabla, right?

TAMARIND

41 East 22nd Street
(Park Avenue South and Broadway) — *Zagat: 25*
212-674-7400 — *www.tamarinde22.com*
Chef: K. P. Singh

No matter where you are in NYC, there is a lot to be said for the location of this top-rated Indian restaurant located half a block from the #6 subway stop on East Twenty-second Street. I mean, you might not feel like going out tonight, and you might not feel like cooking at home or even ordering in, and you can jump on any subway and get to the #6 and eureka! There you are . . . sitting at the fourteen-seat bar, being served the special appetizer of cauliflower (which the two thirty-somethings on my right returned to this restaurant to eat), or enjoying the so-called Indian "street food," which has risen to upscale status at Tamarind. You will be served by the friendliest of waitstaff and bartenders, while you lean back on the padded, backed bar seats and watch the quiet crowd on a Saturday night go by to their more formal tables.

No British Colonial or Buddha statues look in this modern, sophisticated Indian setting with artifacts and fabrics on the pristine white walls. Lighting is perfect with a warm glow to the cream-colored bar area, with a line of reserved tables along the wall in back of the bar, leading to the dining room with space enough between tables so that the noise level was high civility. The chefs are seen through a sparkling-clean glass case that jets out into the main dining room and can be seen from the bar. No loitering on any front in this efficiently smooth, smiling-staffed restaurant.

The regular diners at the tables were dressed more formally than several of the bar diners, who were as comfortable as they should be in jeans. A triangle of white linen served as place mat, and the bartender served each diner from a serving dish brought to the bar. At the end of the bar sat two Woody Allen movie–like women chatting, smiling, thoroughly engaged in their stories. The bar had two couples eating dinner at 8:30 on a Saturday night in May, and the rest having a drink and waiting for a table, and by 10:00, all ten were eating dinner at the bar. All ages, some families, a young Indian man and I happened to be the only solos at the bar, but the bartender said that during the week, many more singles dine at the bar than on a Saturday night. The couple on my left came in after the first couple left for the dining room, and it was their big night out with an eleven-month-old at home. Usually they have dinner reservations because they plan babysitters way in advance with plenty of time to get reservations. But when a grandparent or sister offers to sit at the last minute, they hit the dining at the bar of NYC's celebrity chefs scene.

It was from Stephanie that I learned about the street food appetizer, sharing a bite of theirs, as she had just read an article about it. And it was Bryan who was eager to share tastes, starting with their lentil dip for my garlic naan, which I had before they ordered their entrée, perfect with their drinks. The cauliflower, covered in red something, was an interesting look on my right. Oh, yes . . . the dessert!! The rice pudding was served in a cereal-sized bowl (reminding this Vermonter of childhood daily oatmeal with raisins); think chowder consistency rather than sticky rice pudding, creamy and sweet with a few raisins, pistachios, and almonds in the center. A stunning flavor, consistency, and finish to a spicy dinner. The decaf espresso was bold and perfect. I can't wait for you to come here!

TASTING ROOM

264 Elizabeth Street (Houston and Prince) — *Zagat: 22*
212-358-7831 — *www.thetastingroomnyc.com*
Closed: Sundays and Mondays — *Chef: Colin Alevras*

Expectations are high for a 2007 Zagat 27, and I expected some diners at the bar with twelve seats on a Saturday night in early June, or at least in the lounge area seating twelve without reservations. The only people there were young twenty-somethings, friends of the bartender, who were drinking beer at the bar. And no wonder . . . the Tasting Room had at least six draught beers from sleek, chrome modern spouts, not the usual pub look. I requested a Brooklyn IPA from Michael the bartender, who has been there since the move from First Avenue two years ago. There are always twelve wines by the glass, and as the wine cellar boasts more than 350 American labels, known for a wide price range and also for smaller vineyards—the wine by the glass changes often.

The brown-bag-type place mat was put before me when I asked for a menu. The menu has a tasting and a sharing serving, one that is small-plate, much like an appetizer, and the other to share, which is easy when the tables are so close together, is entrée size. For example, the halibut tartare is $15 for taste and $26 for share. The pork rib roast with a fried duck egg is $17/$30, and the American pigeon is $19/$34 for the two different servings. This was the first time I've ever noticed fluke on a menu and I learned that the Hamptons crowd all eat fluke on Memorial Day weekend if they have a fisherman in the family. And there it was on the menu the week after. It has to be fluke season! Served in a bright green pea sauce over just barely cooked turnip quarters, it was delicious, although the sour, underdone turnips didn't add to the dish, especially in springtime.

The rhubarb cake, the size and shape of a muffin, a very light white cake filled with a sweet rhubarb sauce with a side of ice cream surrounded by fresh, crushed pineapple, was very average. All desserts are $9, and one that caught my eye for another time with friends to share was the white chocolate cheesecake with whipped cream and berries according to the season. If I'm in the neighborhood again, I'll look in first and see if anyone is dining at the bar or at least in the lounge . . . otherwise, I'll skip the whole experience and head back over to the Public for a shout with the Aussie blokes!

TELEPAN

72 West 69th Street
(Columbus Avenue and Central Park West) *Zagat: 24*
212-580-4300 *www.telepan-ny.com*
Chef: Bill Telepan

Lincoln Center attendees and all of you Upper West Side fans have to give thanks that Telepan has arrived in your midst. What a warm and sophisticated town-house restaurant experience it is to walk in and see the semicircular light-wood bar featured smack in the center of the room with booths and tables on each side of it. Not only that, but Telepan got the Best Newcomer restaurant award from Zagat for 2007. Small paintings and large photographs on the green walls set the modern and comfortable ambience. You know you've come to the right place with the first smell and feeling of high energy and the mix of young and middle-aged, with a sprinkling of oldish people who are studying the creative presentation in front of them of starters, small mains, mains, and desserts.

Arriving at the bar at 7 p.m. were several singles, two couples, and me—I was headed for Lincoln Center at 8 p.m. I sat beside a young man, Bobby, from Rochester, New York, who moved to the Big Apple right out of university to be a chef. He is currently a cook at Casa Mono, "the top Spanish restaurant in NYC," he told me—a Zagat 25. Metallic place mat, friendly bartenders, two draught beers, plus bottled beers and about twelve wines by the glass from $8 to $17. The bartender brought me tastes from the chef, a little tray with a taste of vegetables with the accent on parsnip, and a fish tartare served in a Chinese soup spoon, as well as a demitasse cup of pumpkin soup. Regulars sit both in the booths and at the bar.

Looking at the appetizers, the smoked brook trout at $15.50 stole my attention, although I certainly noted the roasted quail and duck with a fig sausage for $12.50. I must try that on my next visit. The smoked trout was presented as a pyramid on a buckwheat bilini covered with horseradish crème fraîche, two pieces of chive standing upright on the side with large chunks of trout, not too smoked, just the best imaginable. I mean, this was some elegant-looking and -tasting appetizer! Not beginning to have time to try the desserts, I did have time to look at the dessert menu and two especially caught my eye—the banana tart with an orange caramel sauce for $11, and listen to this combination, also for $11: ruby red grapefruit granita parfait, with a lemon cream, hazelnuts, and Prosecco. Oh, boy, my friend Lita would love that . . . anything with Prosecco in it.

My bar neighbor Bobby had started with the foie gras, and was now eating large, tender chunks of lamb in a cassoulet and broth. He checked out every ingredient, turned forkfuls over to inspect it all, and was indeed there to learn and appreciate excellent cuisine. He followed his entrée with a sherry custard dessert, which was French in size and exquisite presentation. When he asked for a sherry to go with it, the bartender gave him tastes of several sherries to select from. He told me that his brother is in NYC, a Columbia graduate student in art history and a Marine. His dad is an art dealer, and the men in the family gather at NYC's top-chef restaurants as often as possible. You can imagine that I was as fascinated by my bar neighbor, as is often the case, as I will probably be when I get to Lincoln Center. Five minutes before eight! Gotta run!

TÍA POL

205 Tenth Avenue (22nd and 23rd Streets) *Zagat: 24*
212-675-8805 *www.tiapol.com*
Closed: Monday lunch *Chef: Alex Raij*

With more than one hundred world-class art galleries and top-chef restaurants to match this art and gay center of NYC in the center of West Chelsea, you will find a tiny little place with twenty-five seats at tables, and nine seats at the bar—with a line of people spilling out onto the street to get in. The third visit to the area to gather my tastes and stories, I got smart and went at 5:30 so that I could be assured of a seat at this big-time (if not space) tapas bar. Tía Pol is long and narrow with brick walls, and it's almost safe to say that everyone would rather be at the bar; no matter how crowded it is, it's nothing like being stuffed into those tightly placed tables. Dim lights play into the fever of crowded because it's so good, and even the people who don't think they like tapas are pulled in! It's popular, of course, because the food is exceptional. The husband-wife team of Eder Montero, from the Basque, and Alex Raij have worked hard and built themselves great success through their creative food and top-of-the-line ingredients at very reasonable prices.

An all-Spanish wine list goes with the pride of the Spanish-heritage owners. I had been told by a Spaniard to look for the Tempranillo grape among the rioja wines when choosing one, because it is the major grape in all of the red riojas. It gives the wine aroma, flavor, and delicacy, but it is also the grape that contributes the potential for aging.

Wine in hand, now what to eat. The tapas are priced from $3 for fried chickpeas to $11 for a signature dish, the squid in ink with rice. Many things on the menu are available in tapas size or share size such as the head-on shrimp, and the lamb skewers at $5/$10. There is a pork loin sandwich on a baguette with piquillo peppers and tetilla cheese for $9. And look! Even a brandade, the French dish, and obviously Spanish as well—of salt cod and potato purée at $7. You think that 5:30 is too early for tapas? Let me say that I had plenty of company at 5:30, and by 6:30 the place was in full bloom and waiting. I understand that the time or day of the week doesn't matter, those thirty-nine places are quickly and happily taken.

At Tía Pol, if you have room for it, try the signature fried whitebait, served in a paper-lined glass with a lemon wedge. And those bar neighbors all said that I couldn't leave without the Patatas Bravas, rough-cut crispy fried potatoes with spicy aioli. In addition to the menu, each night there are specials of larger plates such as sweet peppers filled with Spanish potato salad and topped with imported white tuna. Or duck breast, sliced and presented on a white plate with lentil salad dressed with a vinaigrette.

This is a fun place to be at the bar. When you're in Chelsea visiting an art gallery, or if you have dinner plans at a restaurant nearby and want to take your starter course here, you won't be disappointed. If you are dining solo, come to the bar to be entertained by the superb food and the motley group of people from every stereotype that you ever dreamed of. Give it a try; this is New York City's melting process!

TOCQUEVILLE

One East 15th Street
(5th Avenue and Union Square West) *Zagat: 26*
212-647-1515 *www.tocquevillerestaurant.com*
Chef: Marco Moreira

The beautiful red-and-cream-colored wide marble bar, six plush bar seats with backs, and six tables for two along the wall facing the bar (without reservations) is the entryway to this intimate dining room with center chandelier and oil paintings, which looks more like an elegant private dining club than a public restaurant. Tocqueville is named for nineteenth-century writer Alexis de Tocqueville (*Democracy in America,* 1835, 1840), not for the chef, who is Japanese Brazilian, not French. Hence the American and Asian spin on the French

menu. And what a creative menu it is, in terms of how things are put together. For example, the special appetizer of the evening was a soft-shell crab (in season—end of May—*bien sûr*) with a poached egg and smoked bacon. I asked the bartender (who could describe the menu as well as any well-trained waiter) how those things were put together. He said they are separate, the egg overlaid with the bacon strip on the plate, and beside it the soft-shell crab. I asked how the foie gras and diver scallops were prepared together, and he explained that they were separate on the plate, but that the tastes and textures were what the chef has in mind on many of his preparations.

I checked out the dinners of the couple on my left; one had ordered the striped bass for $27 and the other the lamb trio for $38. They had been to Tocqueville before and at the last minute couldn't get reservations and so this was their first experience of dining at the bar, and they were loving it! This couple was eager to tell me what they'd had before and how it is never noisy and tables never crowded at this unique space. Looking over the menu, I spotted what I will have next time . . . I'd start with dandelion velouté if it is still in season, which is in a garlic flan for $18. The appetizers start at $15 for six oysters, and the foie gras is $22. Then, without a doubt, I'd go for the turbot, so seldom seen on an American menu. This was served on a celery root purée, with pickled sweet pear and roasted romanesco, for $36.

I did check out the desserts and couldn't wait to taste something in this intimate ambience. I got to thinking about how this would be my last evening "in the field" before moving back to Vermont from Manhattan to write *Belly Up to the Bar,* and I had just had an appetizer, beer, and entrée at Babbo in order to double-check the crowd on a Thursday night. Looking at the Tocqueville dessert menu, I thought I was still at the Italian restaurant when I read "abricot pizza." Just to show you how bold the chef is about ethnicity, what could be a better example? It was exquisite! A small disk of light pastry dough, almost a mille-feuille consistency, with slices of fresh apricot from the Union Square farmers' market, and a dollop of crème fraîche on top.

If you have not dined at the bar of a celebrity chef, here is the place to start. And if you still have reservations about dining at a bar, then take a lounge table at Tocqueville to see for yourself how much the bar diners are enjoying talking about their dining experiences with one another, and next time, try it yourself! At Tocqueville you can count on exquisite taste, superb food, and gracious service.

TSE YANG

34 East 51st Street (Madison and Park Avenues) *Zagat: 25*
212-688-5447 *www.tseyang.citysearch.com*
Chef: Sam Wu

No Chinese restaurant has a higher Zagat rating in NYC than Tse Yang, a 25. Bartender Louis has been here for twenty-two of the twenty-five years that Tse Yang has been in business. It's the kind of midtown restaurant that has a major business lunch and tourist crowd in this palatial, beautiful Asian garden, calm restaurant with regulars (all oldish, very upscale men). All of you over-fifty women who have reservations about dining at the bar at NYC's celebrity chef restaurants would feel very comfortable at this six-seat bar, where Louis says he can squeeze in two more at the bar when needed. A nonsports TV is of major interest to the regulars who were there on a Sunday evening watching Mike Wallace on *60 Minutes.* Most were dressed for an evening out, even on a Sunday night.

As formal as it appears, Louis's friendly banter and personalized service (serving a drink to a regular before it was ordered, calling his diners by name), reminded me more of a French neighborhood café than anything observed in NYC. He waited with great personal charm on his customers, who appeared to be a very in-crowd with handshakes on the way in and on the way out. Family. Louis was the most interesting ingredient of the evening. The bar had cashews coated with a brown sauce (not spicy) for a snack; there is one Chinese beer—Tsingtao—along with the usual Heineken and Amstel Light, plus many wines by the glass. He explained the menu in his bartender's uniform with a lapel proudly sporting a collection of pins that his regulars had given him over the years, the latest being a gold shoulder braid.

Looking over the menu with appetizers starting at $6.25 for spring and autumn rolls to frog legs for $18, and spare ribs for $12.75, if I were here for an appetizer, I would choose the crab leg salad for $14.25, which the man on my right was eating as he was watching Mike Wallace. The entrées had a few surprises, although the Shanghai duck for $24.50 was no surprise, nor the Peking duck for $52, which Louis told me is a specialty of the house with rave reviews. But a veal fillet with tangy spicy sauce at $26.75 was new to me in a Chinese restaurant, as was the calves' liver for $28.75. But then, I love to be surprised! What's the sense of trying new things and going to new places if it is all as you expect? Speaking of the menu, Louis described the Tse Yang chicken as spicy (I took that to mean hot), but when it arrived, I was surprised because it seemed more American Chinese than anything I had tasted in years. No Midwesterner or Northeasterner would have any trouble with this Chinese menu.

The host, Elaine, said that in this locality, the dining room clientele is usually business lunches and dinners or tourists; they have many, many tourists. Upscale, you will note. I have to add, though, when writing about the bar at Tse Yang, that the bar is a little too high for short people to eat at, but then I remembered that in China, the Chinese pick up their plates to mouth level, and so I got away with that plan. Or so I hope!

UNION SQUARE CAFÉ

21 East 16th Street
(5th Avenue and Union Square West) *Zagat: 27*
212-243-4020 *www.unionsquarecafe.com*
Chef: Michael Romano

I head for the Union Square Café bar, knowing it will be crowded with those who know that eating at the Union Square Café bar is the best dining there is, but oh, look! There's a seat . . . three seats up from the other end of the bar. Not all, but almost everyone at the bar is there for dinner—no doubt about it—it is the liveliest, best food, friendliest bartenders, and most fun place to be any night of the week. I say that Union Square Café is the only bar in town where people wait in the restaurant to get to the bar! Starting right off with Anchor Steam on tap . . . what beer lover could ask for anything more? But if Sierra Nevada or Bass Ale is your favorite, besides their specialties of California wines by the glass, you've got three outstanding beers on tap to start with.

I could have chosen one of six different kinds of oysters. I chose three, followed by an appetizer of pumpkin risotto with sage of such large proportion that, along with dessert, I had plenty of tastes for one evening. And for dessert, I already knew I wasn't going for my usual superb Union Square Café warm banana tart, but for the evening's special, chocolate bread pudding with ice cream.

I sat enjoying the ripe olives served on the bar and tasting the best bread served in NYC dipped in olive oil. The Rockport oysters arrived, not briny enough, but oh, so fresh! The couple beside me on my left each had a soup, and then shared a pasta with sausage. I carried on so about my risotto that the young man said he would like to taste it, and then insisted I try his special pasta. Which is a common event at Union Square—tasting a neighbor's selections. I didn't intend to say anything, but out slipped, "It's my daughter's birthday and she lives in New Zealand." Two minutes later a favorite bartender, Mickey, who has been at Union Square Café for ten years at least, walked to my end of the bar to say, "I understand congratulations are in order for your daughter." It's a friendly place.

Looking down the bar, there were two single men on my

right, one single woman next to them, and couples took all the remaining places—no one was not dining at this bar. When I was finished with my risotto, everything was cheerfully cleared and a clean place napkin brought for the chocolate bread pudding, which was extraordinary. Knowing I could eat only half, I took half off my plate as soon as it was served and offered the other half to the new couple on my left, a man and his Indian wife from the World Bank, just in from Washington. Sharing food at the bar introduces the most delicious conversations. Besides food, our conversation centered around Papua New Guinea, where we three had all lived. In the midst of deep conversation about anthropology and living in PNG, I didn't even notice Mickey coming in after my dessert with a platter of cookies from the chef, with a chocolate sauce spelling "HAPPY BIRTHDAY" on the rim of the plate! Oh Elizabeth—just look at this celebration in your name—here at the bar of Union Square Café this very evening!

VERITAS

43 East 20th Street
(Broadway and Park Avenue South)
212-353-3700

Zagat: 26; Michelin: ★
www.veritas-nyc.com
Chef: Ed Cotton

Veritas. Walk into this austere restaurant, and you will see that the name fits. Latin for "truth": The word so often found in school and university mottos. Another world. A wine world, in fact. Their temperature-controlled cellar houses one hundred thousand bottles of wine, and listen to this, the wine list you will be handed counts three thousand labels. Don't give up! You can ask and you shall receive—all kinds of advice about what to order according to what you feel like this evening.

Ed Cotton has earned a 26 Zagat rating out of the top 28, and a Michelin star. He creates his three-course prix-fixe dinner to go with the wines, rather than the other way around with a balance in mind of meat, fish, and poultry. The warmest part of the restaurant is at the bar, comme habitude, where we found nine very comfortable bar seats, and two together at 8:30 on an October Saturday night. By 10:30 the place was booming, and not a seat at the bar or in the small dining room was to be had. The lighting was perfect and we loved the sound level of civility, because most of us would find it easy to agree that the buzz of a full house is welcomed.

It didn't even cross my mind to ask for the beer list; I was afraid of insulting the wine sommelier with his list of three thousand wines in hand. The beauty of going to the bar, of course, is to have as long a conversation as you want with the bartender until you decide what you want to order. Another beauty of going to the bar is that you can share that prix-fixe menu if you want a late, light dinner. Looking at the short wine list by the glass—there are two champagnes by the glass at \$19 and \$28; five sherries from \$7 to \$11; four whites and four reds from \$12 to \$20. I wanted to try something new, and so after tasting two whites, chose Les Grandes Vignes du Roy, Châteauneuf-du-Pape made from the grenache blanc grape from the southern Rhône region, which was described as a medium-bodied, mineral-laced, and fruit-driven spectacular wine. Phew! That's a lot of info. I thought it sounded like a sauvignon blanc, and I was thrilled when the sommelier agreed, in that he at least could see where I was coming from in the "mineral-laced, fruit-driven" part! Lita loves everything Italian and wanted to try a Piedmont red, so she chose Elio Perrone from the barbera grape, a medium body, with a soft and smoother mouth feel. And yes, we talked more wine than food that evening, and it was very exciting to be in a place that was so happy to explain so much about wine, and to be able to look forward to the food to go with it, as well.

Oh, yes, the food. We looked forward to the three courses and checking out the eight appetizers, which included crisp sweetbreads with caramelized endive, Madeira, and fennel pollen; a wild mushroom ravioli with truffles, tarragon, and chives; we decided to go for the hamachi tartare with fennel purée, cucumber, chilies, and blood orange. Yes! We tasted each of the subtle flavors, loved the hot chilies with the cool cucumber and acid of the orange.

There was a wonderful range of entrées, with a good mix of fish and red meats, and an organic chicken. We took note of the New Zealand red snapper and venison (I notice anything New Zealand with a Kiwi daughter), checked out the roasted saddle of lamb, and Lita graciously agreed that we would skip over that because it was served with chèvre potato purée, which most people would love, but not me! There was also a rib eye steak, but we chose the braised short ribs with a parsnip purée, porcini mushrooms, glazed carrots, and Barolo. It was all that we had hoped for from Ed Cotton.

We almost didn't want to go on to the dessert, as the entrée with the wine was so perfect. But I can't leave out the dessert menu because many of you will like dessert best . . . after the wine, of course. So here are your choices: The chocolate soufflé is served with Thai coffee ice cream and chocolate sauce. A bamboo honey panna cotta is served with almonds, bee pollen, and raspberries; and then there is a warm banana financier with crème fraîche sorbet and macadamia brittle. A toss-up on the last two, but ultimately we went for the raspberry-and-honey combination. Such a satisfying evening at Veritas. When you're in the mood for a 26 in a serene setting, choose truth in wine and food at Veritas!

VONG

200 East 54th Street (3rd Avenue) *Zagat: 22; Michelin: ★*
212-486-9592 *www.jean-georges.com*
Chef: Jean-Georges Vongerichten

Prime sirloin over noodles in a ginger broth? Chicken and chocolate milk soup, gaiangal and shiitake mushrooms? How did the esteemed Jean-Georges get into French-Thai? After learning his craft in France, he worked for several years in Bangkok and *voilà!* You won't find another French-Thai (if you were looking for one, that is) restaurant that has the decor, the designer name, and the exquisite food that you will find at Vong. Entering the restaurant, you will be struck with the calm Asian ambience of the wooden slats, sleek modern wood furniture, and red Thai silk plaid wall hangings that greet you. The Buddha altar displays bowls of the Thai spices that are used so expertly in the cuisine.

In the bar and lounge is a magnificent wall of decoupage, and as soon as you take your seat at the bar and ask for a menu, a bamboo place setting will be put before you. Vong is known for Jean-Georges's use of 150 different Thai herbs and spices with his French technique, which combine to bring us a very creative menu. Being a major fan of this chef, especially of his flagship restaurant Jean Georges on Central Park West, I couldn't wait to get to the bar of Vong, a restaurant that I hadn't been back to in a couple of years. And never at the bar. And here I am with the appetizer temptations priced from $9 for duck or vegetable rolls, to $18 for the lobster and daikon rolls with rosemary and ginger dippings. I had decided to go for an entrée at Vong, and therefore skipped over the appetizer, but the woman next to me told me that she always gets the crab spring rolls with a tamarind dipping sauce. I looked it over and agreed with her that if I were going to have an appetizer, that would be it.

Looking at the menu, I was intrigued by the rabbit curry with braised carrots and gaiangal mushrooms for $29. I'd had wild rabbit with a little shot left in it, I'd had milder farm-raised rabbits, but never had I tasted a rabbit curry, and this was not to be missed! Annie, the fiftysomething woman on my left, had been to Vong many times, and she never has qualms about

being a woman eating at the bar at any of the Jean-Georges restaurants. She encouraged me to be sure and say so in my book because she has a hard time getting any of her women friends to come with her. Annie said that most often she doesn't know when she will finish work at her office, and when she does, she deserves great food, and where else but at the celebrity chef's bar at the last minute? End of discussion.

On my immediate right was a couple in their thirties, and then three solo middle-aged men and a woman. Annie told me that she was on a vegetarian kick (to include fish, though), and had ordered the seared bean curd with a sweet-and-sour mushroom broth. Of course she couldn't very well taste my rabbit curry, being on her vegetarian kick, but I did get to taste the bean curd and liked the rabbit much better. At the same time, we agreed that we could easily share a dessert, and so after much discussion and agreeing that we didn't need to have chocolate, it was easy to order the passion fruit panna cotta in a pineapple broth with yogurt sorbet. Sound nutritious? I want to add that the flavors and textures were as good-tasting as they were good for us! The excitement of the Asian look with palm trees, the Buddah altar, and the superb service all add up to Vong as a destination.

WALLSÉ

344 West 11th Street (Washington Street) — *Zagat: 26; Michelin:* ★
212-352-2300 — *www.wallse.com*
Chef: Kurt Gutenbrunner

Wallsé is one of seven Michelin-one-star restaurants in the West Village. Come on down (or up, for you TriBeCa residents)! Now this is Village, as you out-of-towners imagine Greenwich Village. Small, warm, informal, just perfect for bringing your out-of-town visitor, or for you traveling professionals and businesspeople who are looking for the best of food without reservations and who want that Village feeling. This is one of the few Village places where you can "hear yourself think." This setting, with major black and blue art on the white walls, and the Austrian chef Kurt Gutenbrunner, is where you will find enough regulars who are eager to tell you more about where you are. Thirties-to-seventies mix of ages; the classic Austrian menu is key; the Austrian pastries are signature.

The waitstaff are dressed uniformly in black with long black aprons and are especially helpful and well-schooled in the menu and wine list. A few wines by the glass starting at $7 and champagne at $9, but mostly mixed drinks of all kinds and martinis came out of the bar to every five or six beers. There is a window at the end of the bar, and through it came barrels of ice, more peanuts, and out went bottles of wine and fast talk and flying hands. A young-looking Robert De Niro type assured me that many ate at the bar (no one else was dining from 8:30 to 10 p.m. the night I was there), and that it was the same extraordinary chef, Kurt Gutenbrunner from Bouley, who attracted so many particular diners to this art deco dining room with a Hollywood 1940s look. A few feet away from the bar is a railing, and as many were packed and standing around this area, they hemmed in the ten or so bar tables that ran the length of the bar against the wall that leads to the main

dining room. A waiter found his way to me and asked if he could take my coat; hard to believe he would notice in the crowd and commotion!

At lunch, these tables are clothed in white linen for the luncheon crowd that finds many more dining at the bar on Mr. Gutenbrunner's creations. Deciding I'd do well to last through one Heineken, appetizer, and dessert, I started with the Maine crab and Florida shrimp on a bed of diced cucumber surrounded with asparagus. But first! The familiar triangle of white linen at my place on the bar, dinnerware, and a big silver basket of bread, with at least five kinds of superb rolls of a variety of shapes and flavors. Two circular slabs of butter accompanied the bread, and the appetizer, though beautiful to look at and with not too much dressing, didn't begin to live up to the subtle flavor of Maine crab as anticipated by this diner who had forgotten that Maine crab, like lobster, just isn't worth eating "south of Boston." Just as the recommended apple-and-walnut strudel with vanilla ice cream and schlag appeared, a couple squeezed in—she sat, he stood—and without asking for a menu, they ordered the Wiener schnitzel with potato-cucumber salad. Good! Others do eat at the bar at Wallsé! Next time I think I'll do that—order the Austrian Wiener schnitzel.

WD-50

50 Clinton Street
(Riverton and Stanton Streets)
212-477-2900

Zagat: 23; Michelin: ★
www.wd-50.com
Chef: Wylie Dufresne

Don't ever seek comfort food or mom's home cooking with Mr. wd-50 risk-taker! Do come on down to the Lower East Side if you've tried everything except square oysters, and if you are looking for creative objets d'art on your plate . . . not in the setting. You don't have to like it, you don't have to try it, and that's the beauty of eating at the bar. If you don't know what you are in for, innocently sitting at the very beautiful marble bar (the best-looking part of the restaurant with bottle-shaped drop lamps from the ceiling), looking for roast chicken, have your drink and get up and walk down to Alias at 76 Clinton. Probably half of the people who have tried wd-50 love it, and the other half can't stand it. If you have tried everything, though, except square oysters, and you are an adventuresome soul, then you are in for a treat! Your dining experience at wd-50 will be memorable and a topic of your conversation for weeks to come even in the most chic of NYC circles. To start right off, you should know that Wylie's mission is to serve sophisticated modern American fare in a casual setting. Casual it is. From the street you will see a big black-tinted window within a wooden frame, and a huge wooden door all set in a brick wall. Inside are a few booths after the bar in a long, narrow dining room, followed by modern wooden tables and chairs. Please note, the downstairs restroom is so modern, several of us couldn't find the doors! Over the sinks are a major mosaic of blues and orange of under-the-sea fish by Tim Snell.

Back upstairs at the bar, Kate, a Columbia MFA writing graduate student, and I ventured in without knowing very much about this chef except that Wylie Dufresne is a partner of Jean-Georges, so how wrong could we be? We were not intimidated by the look of the place, and as soon as we sat down and looked at the menu, a plastic woven place mat was set before us. We were very intrigued with the appetizers, which range from $14 to $17, the first being a mussel-olive-oil soup, with water chestnuts and orange powder. We decided to splurge on the foie gras, candied olives, green peas, and beet juice. And we got a look from and a discussion with the young man sitting on my left, who was enjoying the corned duck, with rye crisp, purple mustard, and horseradish cream.

The turbot, salsify, smoked bulgur, and coffee-saffron for $30 was my entrée choice, and here's more for you to consider! The website is fabulous; beside each dish on the menu is a little icon of a camera, which you can click on and see each dish. You may think you are in Chelsea at a world-class art gallery, but you aren't, you are just checking out the menu at wd-50! Go ahead and look, as you know what a picture is worth! Especially look at his renowned dishes, the oyster pearls, as they are called, and the beef tongue, with fried mayo and tomato molasses.

Oh, yes! It's so easy to get carried away with the food, I forgot about the wine list. Even the wine list has a twist; there are as many wines by the glass in the rosé (listed as pink) section as the white and red . . . that's a first! Five in each, and the price range is from $9.50 to $13.50. Kate and I loved it. Now that we know what to expect, I think we'll enjoy it even more

the next time we go. Wylie Dufresne has to think a lot about getting these dishes together, and I have to say, you will have to think a lot about what it will be like. I think the level of trust will probably be higher the second time when you read "mussel-olive-oil soup." Or "parsnip cake"!

WOLFGANG'S STEAKHOUSE

4 Park Avenue (33rd Street) *Zagat: 25*
212-889-3369 *www.wolfgangssteakhouse.com*
Chef: Amiro Cruz

Come to this Murray Hill steak house with thirteen seats at the bar any night of the week just to look at the vaulted ceiling. No kidding! Not some new designer place, but this location is in the 1912 Vanderbilt Hotel dining room, with a mosaic vaulted ceiling, the work of nineteenth-century artist Rafael Guastavino. Wolfgang Zwiener knows the steak business. He was head waiter at Peter Luger in Brooklyn for forty-one years, retired, and couldn't resist starting his own place. He opened a second in TriBeCa, but there's no old Vanderbilt Hotel down there.

The bar and restaurant were jumping with all ages enjoying their prime, dry-aged porterhouse steaks ($37.95), with German, cottage, or steak fries, or mashed or baked potatoes on the side ($10.95). The number one side for vegetables at NYC's top steak houses appears to be spinach: creamed, sautéed, or steamed ($8.95). Options also include sautéed onions, fried onion rings, sautéed mushrooms, or asparagus. Offerings for a starter are oysters on the half shell for $12.95, jumbo shrimp cocktail for $16.95, and we are talking jumbo here, not something to be ordered if you are going on to a huge porterhouse! The crab cake is $16.95. Now if you think that the lobster cocktail, oysters, or clams on the half shell just won't do it, or if the steak isn't going to put enough fat into your daily intake, you could even have extra-thick sizzling Canadian bacon as a starter for $2.95 a slice.

Oh, I forgot . . . there are bowls on the bar of Wolfgang-made warm potato chips for snacking. If you go in very hungry and order a great beer, keep in mind that it will take a lot of self-control to keep those chips down to a minimum in order to enjoy that steak. Now Mr. Wolfgang prides himself on his knowledge of beef. He inspects sides of beef, stores it in his temperature-controlled meat cooler until it is dried and aged to his specifications, and when you get it, sizzling on a platter, you are going to have to have plenty of appetite to eat it all. Not only is there a steak for one, but there is a steak for two, a steak for three at $118.35, and even a steak for four at $157.80. As you reach for another chip, look over at those bar diners diving into their steaks, and you'll be happy to wait for yours.

There seemed to be more women at Wolfgang's than at other steak houses, although no women were dining at the bar at 10 p.m. on this particular Monday night. The friendly bartender says that most of the women are there for business lunches or after-dinner drinks. "There are a lot more men out there who don't want to cook their own dinner when they can be here for a steak," was the experience of this Wolfgang bartender. A midtown steak house in a landmark building with incredible steaks is what is waiting for you at Wolfgang's Park Avenue Steakhouse.

WHAT'S YOUR TASTE?

You are now well aware of the palate, ambience, observations, tastes, and opinions of this writer. Now JSM is eager to hear what you, the bar diner, think, observe, and experience while dining at the bar of NYC's celebrity chefs. Did you find another restaurant's dining bar that you think should be included in the next edition of *Belly Up to the Bar*? Did you go to a bar in this guide that didn't begin to live up to your expectations? Did you find a noise level that is absolutely unacceptable? A chef that can't be beat, no matter what his Zagat or Michelin rating? A bartender who has been there for years and is the best? Then, by all means, send your delicious discoveries from bellying up to the bar to J. S. Mitchell:

E-mail: BellyUpToBarNYC@aol.com
Write: *Belly Up to the Bar,* Cumberland House Publishing, 431 Harding Industrial Drive, Nashville, TN 37211

INDEX BY LOCATION

Greenwich Village East (Between 14th and Houston Streets)

Chelsea (Between 30th and 14th Streets)

Flatiron (Between 30th and 14th Streets)

Union Square (Around 14th Street)

Gramercy Park (Between 30th and 14th Streets)

Midtown West (Between 59th and 30th Streets)

Midtown East (Between 59th and 30th Streets)

Murray Hill (Between 59th and 30th Streets)

Upper West Side (Between 96th and 59th Streets)

Upper East Side (Between 96th and 59th Streets)

INDEX BY MICHELIN STARS

Three Stars

Two Stars

One Star

ABOUT THE AUTHOR

J. S. Mitchell is the author of thirty-five nonfiction books on a wide variety of subjects. A regular diner at the bars in Manhattan's top restaurants, Mitchell has persuaded many a friend to join in on a first bar-dining experience.